KU-712-924

What Christians Believe at a Glance

ROSE
PUBLISHING

Torrance, California

© 2010 Bristol Works, Inc.
Rose Publishing, Inc.
4733 Torrance Blvd., #259
Torrance, California 90503 U.S.A.
Email: info@rose-publishing.com
www.rose-publishing.com

All rights reserved. No part of this publication may be reproduced, stored in a retrieval system, posted on the Internet, or transmitted in any form or by any means without the prior written permission of the publisher. The only exception is brief quotations in printed reviews.

Includes these Rose Publishing Titles:

Essential Doctrine Made Easy © 2007 Norman L. Geisler
        Author: Norman L. Geisler, MA, ThB, PhD
Creeds and Heresies: Then & Now © 2009 Bristol Works, Inc.
        Author: Benjamin Galan, MTS, ThM
The Trinity © 1999, 2005 RW Research, Inc.
        Contributing authors: Robert M. Bowman, Jr., MA; Dennis L. Okholm, PhD;
        Gary M. Burge, PhD; Paul Carden; Robert Cubillos; Ron Rhodes, PhD
Life of Jesus © 2010 Bristol Works, Inc.
Denominations Comparison © 2003, 2005 RW Research, Inc.
        Author: Robert M. Bowman, Jr., MA
        Research consultant: Eric Pement
Baptism © 2008 Bristol Works, Inc.
        Contributing authors: Benjamin Galan, MTS, ThM; William Brent Ashby, BT
Understanding the Book of Revelation © 2009 Bristol Works, Inc.
        Contributing authors: Benjamin Galan, MTS, ThM; William Brent Ashby, BT
What's So Great about Heaven © 2009 Bristol Works, Inc.
        Author: Benjamin Galan, MTS, ThM

Many of these titles are available as individual pamphlets, as wall charts, and as ready-to-use PowerPoint® presentations.

All Scripture quotations, unless otherwise noted, are taken from the *Holy Bible, New International Version*®. *NIV*®. Copyright © 1973, 1978, 1984 by International Bible Society. Used by permission of Zondervan. All rights reserved.

Library of Congress Cataloging-in-Publication Data

What Christians believe at a glance.
        p. cm. – (Rose Bible basics)
Summary: "Summaries and comparisons of basic Christian beliefs on topics such as doctrines, baptism, end times, and life after death"–Provided by publisher.
  ISBN 978-1-59636-414-1 (pbk.)
  1. Theology, Doctrinal–Popular works. I. Rose Publishing (Torrance, Calif.)
  BT77.W47 2010
  230–dc22
                                        2010007773

Printed by Regent Publishing Services Ltd.
Printed in China
April 2010, First printing

What
Christians Believe
at a Glance

Contents

Continued
on next
page

→

What
Christians Believe
at a Glance

Contents

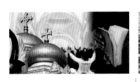

Essential Doctrine
Made Easy

16 Key Christian Beliefs

What Do Christians Believe?

What are the key doctrines of the Christian faith? The core teachings of the Bible have defined Christianity for 2,000 years. Virtually all Christians who seek to have a faith that is biblical hold to some form of these basic doctrines. Christians may not always agree on how they work out the details of their faith, but they should agree on the essential doctrines, these core truths.

In essentials, unity; in non-essentials, liberty, and in all things, charity.[1]

We can identify the essential doctrines of the Christian faith by looking at the core truth of the gospel, which is the salvation of humanity through the life, death, and resurrection of Jesus Christ. Salvation, as God has revealed to us through his Holy Scriptures, is defined as forgiveness of sins and everlasting life with God by confessing that "Jesus is Lord" and believing that God raised Jesus from the dead (Romans 10:9). By examining the gospel message, we can identify 14 doctrines that are necessary for salvation to be possible.

What Are the Essential Doctrines?

The essential doctrines of Christianity have to do with

➤   who God is,
➤   who Jesus Christ is,
➤   God's love for people, and his desire to save them.

Below are the 14 essential salvation doctrines that have to be true in order for anyone to know God and be saved:

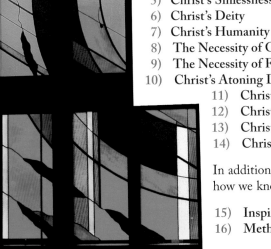

1) God's Unity
2) God's Tri-unity
3) Human Depravity
4) Christ's Virgin Birth
5) Christ's Sinlessness
6) Christ's Deity
7) Christ's Humanity
8) The Necessity of God's Grace
9) The Necessity of Faith
10) Christ's Atoning Death
11) Christ's Bodily Resurrection
12) Christ's Bodily Ascension
13) Christ's Intercession
14) Christ's Second Coming

In addition, two more essentials define how we know about salvation:

15) Inspiration of Scripture
16) Method of Interpretation

1 GOD'S UNITY

There is only one God. He has always existed and will always exist. There is one— and only one—God, Creator of the universe.

What Do I Actually Need to Believe?
There is only one God.

What's at Stake Here?
Knowing the only true God (John 17:3).

Hear O Israel: The LORD our God, the LORD is one.
—Deuteronomy 6:4

I am the LORD your God.… You shall have no other gods before me. —Exodus 20:2–3

Before me no god was formed, nor will there be one after me. I, even I, am the LORD and apart from me there is no savior. —Isaiah 43:10–11

2 GOD'S TRI-UNITY

While there is only one God, he exists eternally in three Persons. In the Bible:

➤ the Father is called God,
   (2 Thessalonians 1:2)
➤ the Son (Jesus) is called God,
   (John 1:1–5; 10:30–33; 20:28; Hebrews 1:8; Philippians 2:9–11)
➤ the Holy Spirit is called God.
   (Acts 5:3–4; 2 Corinthians 3:17)

He is one substance but three Persons in relationship. There are more than 60 passages in the Bible that mention the three Persons together.

What Do I Actually Need to Believe?
God is one essence, but three Persons.

What's at Stake Here?
The unity and relational nature of God.

As soon as Jesus was baptized, he went up out of the water. At that moment heaven was opened, and he saw the Spirit of God descending like a dove and lighting on him. And a voice from heaven said, "This is my Son, whom I love; with him I am well pleased." —Matthew 3:16–17

Therefore go and make disciples of all nations, baptizing them in the name of the Father and of the Son and of the Holy Spirit. —Matthew 28:19

May the grace of the Lord Jesus Christ, and the love of God, and the fellowship of the Holy Spirit be with you all. —2 Corinthians 13:14

HUMAN DEPRAVITY

Since God is a personal Being, he wants personal relationships with human beings. Human depravity means that every human is spiritually separated from God, totally incapable of saving himself. When Adam sinned, he died spiritually and his relationship with God was severed. Additionally, all of Adam's descendants are "dead in transgressions" (Ephesians 2:1). Without a new birth (being created anew) no one can enter life (John 3:3).

What Do I Actually Need to Believe?

We are sinful and cannot please God by our own good works alone. We can never be "good enough."

What's at Stake Here?

When we try to deal with the problem of separation and death on our own terms, we will fail, resulting in eternal separation from God.

As it is written: "There is no one righteous, not even one; there is no one who understands, no one who seeks God. All have turned away, they have together become worthless; there is no one who does good, not even one."
—Romans 3:10–11

CHRIST'S VIRGIN BIRTH

Jesus was born as a result of a miracle: Mary, Jesus' mother, became pregnant without ever having sexual relations. The doctrine of Jesus' Virgin Birth is not primarily about Mary's virginity and miraculous conception. Though this miracle fulfilled a preordained prophecy (Isaiah 7:14), the reason it is essential has to do with God's supernatural intervention. Our sin is not merely something we do—it is who we are. It is inborn. Our depravity is transmitted to us from our parents (Psalm 51:5; 1 Corinthians. 15:22; Romans 5:12-15). Because God interrupted the natural birth process in the case of Jesus, Jesus did not inherit a sin nature. In other words, Jesus not only did not sin, he had no inclination to sin even when tempted. He was perfect.

What Do I Actually Need to Believe?

Jesus became a human being through a supernatural conception in Mary's womb.

What's at Stake Here?

God's supernatural intervention in order to break the chain of sin.

This is how the birth of Jesus Christ came about: His mother Mary was pledged to be married to Joseph, but before they came together, she was found to be with child through the Holy Spirit…. [An angel said]: "Joseph son of David, do not be afraid to take Mary home as your wife, because what is conceived in her is from the Holy Spirit. She will give birth to a son, and you are to give him the name Jesus, because he will save his people from their sins." All this took place to fulfill what the Lord had said through the prophet: "The virgin will be with child and will give birth to a son, and they will call him Immanuel"—which means, "God with us."
—Matthew 1:18–23

5 CHRIST'S SINLESSNESS

Christ was born of a virgin, and he did not suffer the effects of a sin nature. Throughout his life Jesus remained sinless. Because of our sin, we could not have a relationship with God; but because Jesus did not sin he was perfectly able to represent us (stand in our place) before God.

What Do I Actually Need to Believe?

Jesus was perfect.

What's at Stake Here?

The ability of Christ to represent us before God and thus provide salvation for us.

God made him who had no sin to be sin for us, so that in him we might become the righteousness of God. —2 Corinthians 5:21

We have one who has been tempted in every way, just as we are—yet was without sin. —Hebrews 4:15

He committed no sin, and no deceit was found in his mouth. —1 Peter 2:22

6 CHRIST'S DEITY

The only way for humans to be restored spiritually to God was for God to build a bridge across the gap of separation. So God, while retaining his full God nature, became a perfect man in Christ in order to bridge the chasm. If he is not both God and Man, he cannot mediate between God and man (1 Timothy 2:5). Jesus Christ is the second Person in the Trinity.

What Do I Actually Need to Believe?

Jesus Christ is, in essence, God. He is divine, not just a good teacher or a righteous man.

What's at Stake Here?

Jesus' ability to save us.

In the beginning was the Word, and the Word was with God, and the Word was God. —John 1:1

For in Christ all the fullness of the deity lives in bodily form. —Colossians 2:9

But about the Son he says, "Your throne, O God, will last for ever and ever." —Hebrews 1:8

7 CHRIST'S HUMANITY

Jesus was also fully human. Jesus got tired; he slept; he sweated; he got hungry and thirsty. Without being fully human, Jesus could not pay the price for human sin. He needed to be divine to have the power to *save* us, and he needed to be human in order to adequately *represent* us. Christ had to be both divine and human.

What Do I Actually Need to Believe?
Jesus Christ was fully human, as well as fully divine.

What's at Stake Here?
Confidence in Jesus' ability to fully represent humankind in atonement.

The Word became flesh and made his dwelling among us. —John 1:14

Christ Jesus ... taking the very nature of a servant, being made in human likeness. —Philippians 2:7–8

Since the children have flesh and blood, he too shared in their humanity so that by his death he might destroy him who holds the power of death—that is, the devil. —Hebrews 2:14

8 THE NECESSITY OF GOD'S GRACE

Because of human depravity, we cannot save ourselves. It is by God's grace alone that salvation is possible. God is right to call humankind to account for sin. However, by his grace, undeserving people will be united in fellowship with him and avoid judgment. Without God's grace, no one could come into relationship with God. Relationship with God is peace, joy, and eternal life itself (John 17:3).

What Do I Actually Need to Believe?
God—and God alone—is able to rescue us.

What's at Stake Here?
Our relationship to God, eternal life.

For it is by grace you have been saved, through faith—and this not from yourselves, it is the gift of God—not by works, so that no one can boast. —Ephesians 2:8–9

If a man remains in me and I in him, he will bear much fruit; apart from me you can do nothing. —John 15:5

He saved us, not because of righteous things we had done, but because of his mercy. —Titus 3:5–7

It does not, therefore, depend on man's desire or effort, but on God's mercy. —Romans 9:16

9 THE NECESSITY OF FAITH

Faith is trusting that God can and will save us. No one can earn salvation. No amount of good works can ever repay the debt that is owed to God. However, by trusting in him and thankfully accepting his gift of salvation, we can be united with God. Faith is an act on our part, but it is not a work. Faith is trusting God to do what we could not do for ourselves (Ephesians 2:8–9; Titus 3:5).

What Do I Actually Need to Believe?
That faith, not works, connects us to God.

What's at Stake Here?
Whether we want to be judged by what we deserve or with God's undeserved favor (grace).

And without faith it is impossible to please God, because anyone who comes to him must believe that he exists and that he rewards those who earnestly seek him.
—Hebrews 11:6

However, to the man who does not work but trusts God who justifies the wicked, his faith is credited as righteousness.   —Romans 4:5

10 CHRIST'S ATONING DEATH

The penalty for sin is death—not only physical death (separation of the soul from the body), but also spiritual death (separation of ourselves from God). The penalty we owe to God was paid by Christ through his death on the cross. The acceptable payment had to be perfect, complete, and without fault. Christ, the perfect human, gave himself in our place, so that whoever believes in him will not die (physically and spiritually) but have everlasting life (John 3:16).

What Do I Actually Need to Believe?
Only Christ's sinless life, sacrificial death, and bodily resurrection can bring us to God.

What's at Stake Here?
The unique nature of Jesus' work of salvation.

For even the Son of Man did not come to be served, but to serve, and to give his life as a ransom for many.   —Mark 10:45

He himself bore our sins in his body on the tree, so that we might die to sins and live for righteousness.   —1 Peter 2:24

For Christ died for sins once for all, the righteous for the unrighteous, to bring you to God.
—1 Peter 3:18

No one comes to the Father except through me.   — John 14:6

11 CHRIST'S BODILY RESURRECTION

The atoning death of Christ paid for our sins, but the process was not complete until he had defeated death by being physically resurrected in the same body (John 2:19-21). Because Christ is the victor over death and the prototype of a new, glorified physical body, all of humanity will be resurrected and live forever in either heaven or hell.

What Do I Actually Need to Believe?
Jesus rose bodily from the grave.

What's at Stake Here?
The proof that Jesus conquered death.

He was delivered over to death for our sins and was raised to life for our justification.
—Romans 4:25

If you confess with your mouth, "Jesus is Lord," and believe in your heart that God raised him from the dead, you will be saved.   —Romans 10:9

Jesus said to them ... "Touch me and see; a ghost does not have flesh and bones, as you see I have.   —Luke 24:38–39

12 CHRIST'S BODILY ASCENSION

Christ died for our sins and was physically resurrected for our salvation. Then 40 days later, he was taken up ("ascended") bodily into heaven. Because Christ has ascended to the Father, the Holy Spirit now guides us, shows us where we are wrong, and comforts us when we hurt. Jesus' going to the Father means our life is kept safe in heaven with God.

What Do I Actually Need to Believe?
Jesus ascended, body and soul, to God.

What's at Stake Here?
The Holy Spirit's work in the life of the believer.

But I tell you the truth: It is for your good that I am going away. Unless I go away, the Counselor [Holy Spirit] will not come to you; but if I go, I will send him to you.   —John 16:7

When he had led them out to the vicinity of Bethany, he lifted up his hands and blessed them. While he was blessing them, he left them and was taken up into heaven.   —Luke 24:50–51

After he said this, he was taken up before their very eyes, and a cloud hid him from their sight. They were looking intently up into the sky as he was going.   —Acts 1:9–10

13 CHRIST'S INTERCESSION

Christ's bodily ascension allowed him to serve as our mediator (or high priest) before God. In God's presence, Christ prays continually on our behalf. As a lawyer defends someone before a judge, so Jesus defends us before the bar of God's law and against the accusations of Satan (Revelation 12:10).

What Do I Actually Need to Believe?
Christ represents our best interests before God.

What's at Stake Here?
Assurance that my prayers are heard by God.

After he had provided purification for sins, he sat down at the right hand of the Majesty in heaven.   —Hebrews 1:3

For we do not have a high priest who is unable to sympathize with our weaknesses, but we have one who has been tempted in every way, just as we are—yet without sin.   —Hebrews 4:15

Therefore he is able to save completely those who come to God through him, because he always lives to intercede for them.
    —Hebrews 7:25

But if anybody does sin, we have one who speaks to the Father in our defense—Jesus Christ, the Righteous One.   —1 John 2:1

14 CHRIST'S SECOND COMING

Just as Christ left the world physically, so he will return in the same manner. His second coming is the hope of the world. When he returns, dead believers will receive their resurrected bodies. Believers that are alive when he returns will not die, but will be transformed into immortal, physical bodies. Christ's bodily return to earth will be visible to all, and believers will rule with him in his kingdom and live with him forever. Those who do not believe will be separated from God's goodness forever.

What Do I Actually Need to Believe?
Jesus is coming again soon, and we should be ready.

What's at Stake Here?
Our hope of being together with Christ.

At that time the sign of the Son of Man will appear in the sky, and all the nations of the earth will mourn. They will see the Son of Man coming on the clouds of the sky, with power and great glory.   —Matthew 24:30

Behold, I am coming soon! My reward is with me, and I will give to everyone according to what he has done.   —Revelation 22:12

For you died, and your life is now hidden with Christ in God. When Christ, who is your life, appears, then you also will appear with him in glory.   —Colossians 3:3–4

You also must be ready, because the Son of Man will come at an hour when you do not expect him.   —Luke 12:40

After Jesus returns, believers will enter conscious eternal blessing and unbelievers will go into conscious eternal punishment.

Eternal Life

Do not let your hearts be troubled. Trust in God; trust also in me. In my Father's house are many rooms; if it were not so, I would have told you. I am going there to prepare a place for you. And if I go and prepare a place for you I will come back and take you to be with me that you also may be where I am.   —John 14:1–3

Now we see but a poor reflection as in a mirror; then we shall see face to face. Now I know in part; then I shall know fully, even as I am fully known.   —1 Corinthians 13:12

He will wipe every tear from their eyes. There will be no more death or mourning or crying or pain, for the old order of things has passed away.   —Revelation 21:4

Eternal Separation

This will happen when the Lord Jesus is revealed from heaven in blazing fire with his powerful angels. He will punish those who do not know God and do not obey the gospel of our Lord Jesus. They will be punished with everlasting destruction and shut out from the presence of the Lord and from the majesty of his power.   —2 Thessalonians 1:7–9

Then I saw a great white throne and him who was seated on it. Earth and sky fled from his presence, and there was no place for them. And I saw the dead, great and small, standing before the throne…. The dead were judged according to what they had done…. Then death and Hades were thrown into the lake of fire. If anyone's name was not found written in the book of life, he was thrown into the lake of fire.   —Revelation 20:11–15

How Do We Know about Essential Doctrines?

We know about the essential doctrines through the Bible; however, the inspiration of Scripture as a doctrine is not necessary for salvation to be possible. People were saved before there was a Bible, and some people are saved without ever reading the Bible. The Bible is, however, the only divinely authoritative foundation that makes the plan of salvation *knowable*.

15 INSPIRATION OF SCRIPTURE

In order for us to have a sure foundation for what we believe, God revealed his Word (the Bible) as the basis of our beliefs. As Thomas Aquinas put it, "in order that salvation might the easier be brought to man and be more certain, it was necessary that men be instructed concerning divine matters through divine revelation"[2] which is the Bible. God cannot err (Hebrews 6:18) and neither can his Word (John 17:17). Without a divinely authoritative revelation from God, such as we have in the Scriptures, we could never be sure of the doctrines that are necessary for salvation.

16 METHOD OF INTERPRETATION

In addition, all the salvation doctrines are derived from the Bible by the literal method of interpretation—that is, Scripture is true, just as the author meant it. By applying the historical-grammatical method of interpretation to Scripture one can know *which* truths are essential for salvation.

To Believe or Not to Believe?

Not all doctrines necessary for salvation are necessary for a person to believe in order to be saved. There is a distinct difference between what must be *true* in order for us to be saved and what must be *believed* in order for us to be saved. For instance, nowhere does the Bible say it is necessary to believe in the Virgin Birth in order to get into heaven; nonetheless, the Virgin Birth assures us that God took an active role in breaking the bonds of sin through his Son, Jesus.

There are certain essential doctrines that one may not believe and still be saved (for example, the Virgin Birth, Ascension of Christ, the Second Coming), and there are certain things one *must* believe in order to be saved. A person must believe that Christ died for sins and rose again (Romans 10:9; 1 Corinthians 15:1-6). One must "believe in the Lord Jesus Christ" (Acts 16:31). Since the word "Lord" (*kurios*) when it refers to Christ in the New Testament means "deity," one cannot deny the deity of Christ and be saved (Acts 2:21, 36; 3:14-16; 5:30-35; 10:39; 1 Corinthians 12:3).

If you confess with your mouth, "Jesus is Lord," and believe in your heart that God raised him from the dead, you will be saved. For it is with your heart that you believe and are justified, and it is with your mouth that you confess and are saved. As the Scripture says, "Anyone who trusts in him will never be put to shame." —Romans 10: 9–11

Terms & Definitions

Ascension—Being taken up; Christ was taken up by God into heaven after the resurrection.

Atonement—To cover, cancel, or forgive sins.

Creed—Summary of beliefs or faith statements held in common by a group.

Deity—Godhood; having the nature of God.

Depravity—Humans' natural bent toward sin (see Genesis 3; 1 Corinthians 15:22; Romans 5:12–15).

Doctrine—Formal teaching.

Eternal—Forever; outside of time and space.

Grace—Undeserved favor; God's mercy.

High Priest—One who represents the people of God to God. In ancient Israel, there was only one high priest chosen to represent the entire nation before God in worship. (See *Mediator*.)

Historical-grammatical method—Method of interpreting Scripture which centers on the historical context and the grammatical interpretation of a text.

Incarnation—Jesus' assumption of human nature; his becoming a human being in a specific time and place.

Inspiration (of Scripture)—Supernatural influence that gives God's authority to a human writing.

Intercession—Prayer or intervention on behalf of another.

Mediator—Go-between; one who intervenes between two parties to bring reconciliation.

Orthodoxy—"Right belief" as opposed to "heresy" (wrong belief).

Prophecy—To accurately predict an event or situation.

Redemption—To buy back or redeem.

Resurrection—God's action in bringing a dead body back to life.

Righteousness—Being in right relationship with God and humanity.

Salvation—God's work that delivers us from the consequences of our sin.

Sin—To "miss the mark"; failing. A deviation or transgression of God's will.

Rebellion—The condition of fallen humanity (depravity); a willful transgression of a known law of God. It is what separates humankind from God and reaps the result o of guilt and eternal condemnation. "The wages of sin is death" (Romans 6:23).

Soteriology—Branch of theology dealing with the doctrine of salvation.

Trinity or Tri-unity—Tri = three; unity = one. Describes the nature of the one God who is also three Persons.

[1] Rupertus Meldenius (AD 1627)

[2] (Summa Theologica 1.1.1)

Resources

Bettenson, Henry and Chris Maunder, eds. *Documents of the Christian Church.* 3rd Edition. New York: Oxford University Press, 1999.

Enns, Paul. *Moody Handbook of Theology.* Chicago: Moody, 1989.

Geisler, Norman L. *Systematic Theology*, Vol. 1. *Prolegomena and Bibliology.* Minneapolis: Bethany House Pub., 2002.

_____. *Systematic Theology*, Vol. 2. *God and Creation.* Minneapolis: Bethany House Pub., 2003.

_____. *Systematic Theology*, Vol. 3. *Sin and Salvation.* Minneapolis: Bethany House Pub., 2004.

_____. *Systematic Theology*, Vol. 4. *Church and Last Things.* Minneapolis: Bethany House Pub., 2005.

House, H. Wayne. *Charts of Christian Theology & Doctrine.* Grand Rapids: Zondervan, 1992.

Ryrie, Charles. *Survey of Bible Doctrine.* Chicago: Moody, 1989.

Schaff, Philip. *Creeds of Christendom.* Vol. 2. *Greek and Latin Creeds.* New York: Harper & Brothers, 1931.

Norman L. Geisler, MA, ThB, PhD, professor of Apologetics and Theology at Veritas Evangelical Seminary. He is author of numerous books on apologetics and theology.

Creeds & Heresies:
Then & Now

How Early Christians Defended the Gospel

The Apostles' Creed

The Nicene Creed

The Chalcedonian Creed

Gnosticism

WHERE DID THE CREEDS COME FROM?

As the gospel spread in the first centuries after Jesus' death and resurrection, people wondered about the beliefs of this new religion. Like today, believers then needed quick, accessible answers to questions. Early Christians formulated simple creeds that expressed essential Christian beliefs. These creeds served at least three purposes:

1. *Explanation of the faith*. Creeds are basic, memorable statements of belief.

2. *Training of believers*. Creeds help believers understand who they are, what they believe, and how they should act as Christians. They are like posts that delimit the boundaries of what it means to be, to believe, and live as Christians.

3. *Identification and correction of false teachings:* Even in the first century AD, false teachers abounded—teachers who claimed to follow Jesus but who promoted a message about Jesus that differed radically from the historical accounts proclaimed by apostolic eyewitnesses. Early Christian creeds helped believers to distinguish the truth about Jesus from the alternative perspectives presented by false teachers.

WHAT DOES A CHRISTIAN BELIEVE?

Early Christians struggled to keep their faith rooted in the historical truth about Jesus Christ—a truth first proclaimed by apostolic eyewitnesses, then passed on through oral traditions, and recorded in the New Testament writings. By providing brief summaries of the truth about Jesus, creeds promoted unity and identity among believers in Jesus Christ.

Caravaggio: Crucifixion of St. Peter, Santa Maria del Popolo, Rome

RELIGIOUS PERSECUTION

Jesus Christ is the fulfillment of God's promises to the people of Israel. For this reason, Christianity was not simply another Jewish sect like the Pharisees and Sadducees. Early Christian writings, including the earliest of the creeds, clearly reflect efforts to demonstrate that Christian faith consummated and fulfilled the Old Testament promises of a Messiah. Eventually, this radical claim led to a separation between the church and mainstream Judaism. Some Jewish religious leaders persecuted believers in Jesus. One of these religious leaders—Saul, later known as Paul—eventually trusted Jesus as his Lord and Messiah.

DOCTRINE: From the Latin word *doctrina*, meaning "teaching, learning." A doctrine is a belief that a group holds as true. Christian doctrines organize and explain the beliefs the church learns from the Bible.

CREED: From the Latin word *credo*, meaning "I believe." Creeds are simple summaries of beliefs. They are easy to memorize and flexible to teach.

POLITICAL PERSECUTION

The early church also experienced persecution from the Roman Empire. The Romans were tolerant of other people's religions to a point; because of their respect for ancient and venerable traditions, the Romans even tolerated the Jewish religion. As persecution drove believers away from Jerusalem, it became clear that Christianity was not simply another Jewish sect, and the Romans began to demand that Christians worship the Roman emperor. Christians refused to worship the Emperor and declared that Jesus alone is Lord. Christians' refusal to worship the Emperor was one reason for the vicious Roman persecution in the latter half of the first century. The powerful influences of pagan culture—both in the state religion of emperor worship and in the growing presence of Gnosticism—made it all the more important to articulate clearly what Christians ought to believe. Identifying God as the sole Creator of all things and declaring Jesus as the only Lord became an important confession for the early church.

CONFESSING THE GOOD NEWS

Jesus' life and ministry challenged Jewish expectations and hopes. The radical call to be transformed by the power of the Holy Spirit and live a different life is not easy to digest. New Testament writers had to stretch their knowledge and understanding. These Spirit-inspired authors presented the truth about Jesus in ways that could be understood not only by Jewish people but also in the broader Greco-Roman world and beyond. The New Testament writings and the creeds of early Christianity answered some of the challenges of the Greco-Roman world.

Today, the creeds still give us identity as Christians. They tell us the following and much more:

- What does it mean to be a Christian?
- Why is it important to believe in the Trinity?
- Why is it important that Jesus is fully God and fully human?
- What unites us as believers?

The Apostle Paul emphasizes "one Lord, one faith, one baptism" (Eph. 4:2). When we recite the creeds, we agree with them; and this agreement joins us in one Lord—the God of the Bible, revealed to humanity as one God in three persons—and one faith: the confession of our common belief. The creeds identify us as the church, the called-out people of God.

CONFESSION: From the Latin word *confiteri*, meaning "acknowledge." Like creeds, confessions are an active acknowledgement of the church's faith and teachings. Often, "confessions of faith" include not only creedal declarations but also statements that summarize the unique teachings of a particular denomination or group of believers.

CREEDS IN THE BIBLE

The Bible is a confessional document. It is God's revelation of God's plans for humanity. It also includes human responses to God's revelation: praises (psalms), confessions (for example, Naaman's and Peter's in 2 Kings 5:15 and Matthew 16:16), petitions, and creeds. To treat the Bible as a confessional document means that Christians affirm (confess) its teachings as truthful. These confessions identify Christians as God's people.

BIBLE	SUMMARY	IMPORTANCE TODAY
Deuteronomy 6:4–5 (*Shema*) *Hear, O Israel: The Lord our God, the Lord is one.*	In the midst of peoples with many gods, the *Shema* sets the Israelites apart. It expresses the basic belief about the uniqueness of God.	We live in a world in which many different gods claim people's allegiance. The confession of the *Shema* sets Christians apart by their belief in the one true God.
Romans 10:9 *If you confess with your mouth, "Jesus is Lord," and believe in your heart that God raised him from the dead, you will be saved.*	This passage is a brief summary of a basic Christian belief: the confession that Jesus is Lord as a public testimony of faith.	This text declares the Lordship of Jesus. Jesus is both our one God and our Master. He has proven his divinity and power through his resurrection.
1 Corinthians 15:3–4 *For what I received I passed on to you as of first importance: that Christ died for our sins according to the Scriptures....*	This confession about Jesus' resurrection captures the centrality of the resurrection for the believer.	As the Apostle Paul wrote, if Jesus was not raised from the dead, our faith is in vain (15:17).

HERESY: From the Greek word *hairesis*, meaning "choice." It refers to teachings that contradict another teaching that has been accepted as the norm. Many heretics in the early church began as believers trying to understand difficult teachings about the Trinity (three persons in one perfect divine unity) and the Incarnation (the embodiment of God the Son in human flesh).

ORTHODOX: From the Greek words *ortho*, "straight," and *doxa*, "belief, opinion." Irenaeus coined the word *orthodox* to characterize his own teachings, which most other Church Fathers agreed with, and the word *heresy* to define those of his adversaries.

WHAT DOES A CHRISTIAN NOT BELIEVE?

Creeds are constant reminders of what is central to our faith. Creeds are also boundary markers that set the rules for intelligent, creative conversation about God and his creation. Like fences, creeds protect us from "heresy"—choosing to wander away from the historical testimony about the nature and workings of God found in Holy Scripture.

The creeds of the early church—the Apostolic, Nicene, Athanasian, and Chalcedonian creeds—were responses to heretical teachings. The heresies in the early church were, for the most part, related to our understanding of God and Jesus. Studying the creeds helps us understand the heresies of the past. By understanding those heresies, it is easier to avoid repeating them today.

GNOSTICISM

One ancient and important heresy that still thrives today is Gnosticism. The word *Gnosticism* is derived from the Greek word *gnosis*, meaning "knowledge." Gnosticism emphasized secret knowledge and secret rituals. Salvation consisted of experiencing the secret knowledge and rituals.

Ancient Gnosticism incorporated many beliefs from different religions. As Christianity spread throughout the Roman Empire, Gnostics quickly adopted some Christian practices and terminology. However, Gnosticism completely contradicts Christianity and opposes the biblical understanding of creation and God himself.

In the first two centuries AD, Justin Martyr, Irenaeus, Tertullian, Eusebius, and many others challenged specific forms of Gnosticism and wrote powerful critiques to demonstrate how Gnosticism contradicted biblical Christianity. Partly due to the Gnostic heresy, these three areas became critical for the early church to define:

- The books of the New Testament
- Salvation
- The nature and work of Jesus

TOPIC	GNOSTIC BELIEF	BIBLICAL BELIEF
Cosmogony (Origin of the universe)	A form of pantheism—a belief that identifies God with the universe. God and creation are one. The material world flows out of the divine essence. However, this god is not the God of the Bible, but a fallen god.	God created all things. The Creator and the creation are separate.
Cosmology (Nature, order, and function of the universe)	God is real, but the material world is an illusion. The material world is evil. The human soul, a remnant of the divine, is imprisoned in the body, which is part of the evil world. Humans have forgotten about their divine inner being.	The material world is as real as God. The world is not evil—God called it *good* and *blessed* it.
Origin of Evil	One dominant form of Gnosticism was based on the myth of Sophia, who lusted after the "First Father." Matter is the fruit of her sin. The physical world is evil.	Human sin originates with pride and disobedience. Creation is not evil, although it has been corrupted as a result of human sin.
Salvation	Salvation comes through experiential knowledge—a secret knowledge that teaches one how to escape the evil of a physical world. Its ultimate goal is a return to the original condition of being one with the First Father. In Christian-influenced Gnosticism, Jesus is the one teaching this secret knowledge. The knowledge of people's divine inner being is the main secret knowledge.	God is rescuing humanity through the work of Jesus, not through any special, hidden knowledge.
Jesus	Jesus is not really a human at all; he just appeared to be one. He was an *aeon*, an intermediary between the real world (the world of the spirit) and this evil reality, the material world.	He is the second person of the Trinity. He was incarnated as a real, full human, who atoned for the sins of humanity on the cross.

Gnosticism became such an influential belief system that it has continued to appear over the centuries in people's ideas about God and the world. Much of today's popular spirituality is Gnostic in its orientation.

THE APOSTLES' CREED

© Leah-Anne Thompson

The Apostles did not write the Apostles' Creed. No one knows for certain when this creed was written. References to and quotation of similar statements—known as the "Rule of Faith"—can be found in writings as early as the second century AD. The name "Apostles' Creed" means that the creed contains the Apostolic tradition. The Apostles' Creed is the most universal of all the creeds. Most Christian denominations continue to recite and teach it.

Early creedal statements were very helpful for new Christians in understanding their faith. These early creedal statements were used in baptism. New believers memorized and studied them before being baptized. It is quite possible that from these baptismal "formulas," the ancient church developed what we now call the Apostles' Creed.

TRADITION When contemporary Christians speak of *tradition*, they may mean a human teaching that is not found in the Bible; in this sense, traditions cannot have the same authority as the Bible.

The early church did not use the word *tradition* in this way. The Apostle Paul wrote, "Stand firm and hold to the teachings [or *traditions*] we passed on to you, whether by word of mouth or by letter" (2 Thess. 2:15). *Tradition* meant the handing down of the Apostles' teachings. For the earliest church, the Scriptures were the Old Testament books—the New Testament did not yet have a final form.

Around one hundred years after the death of Jesus, Gnostics produced many writings similar to those in our New Testament; some of those writings claimed to have apostolic authorship—these writings are called the "Gnostic Gospels." The church realized the need to identify and make official the writings that faithfully contained the Apostles' teachings. This became urgent when the influential heretic Marcion questioned the authority of most writings that church fathers accepted.

MARCIONISM Marcion was born around AD 85 and was condemned around AD 144. Marcion rejected the Old Testament. He taught that the God of the Old Testament was angry and vengeful. He taught that the Old Testament God had nothing to do with the God of the New Testament, who is loving and forgiving. Marcion even threw out all writings that agreed, quoted, or referenced the Old Testament! Marcion rejected the Epistle of James and all the other books except Luke and the Pauline epistles. Marcion had rejected the full Apostolic teaching, so the church rejected Marcion's teachings.

APOSTLES' CREED	SUMMARY OF MEANING
I believe in... (Isa. 44:6)	The basic meaning of *creed*. It expresses the beliefs that unite all Christians. The words that follow preserve the teaching of the Apostles.
God, the Father Almighty (Isa. 44:6)	Not just belief in an impersonal force or in many gods, but rather, a deep trust in a personal, caring, loving God.
Maker of heaven and earth. (Gen. 1:1; John 1:1)	God is powerful. Just as God created the universe, God can heal, save, guard, comfort, and guide us. The whole universe is his.
And in Jesus Christ, his only Son, (John 9:38; 20:28)	We believe Jesus is the promised Messiah. Believing in God is also believing in Jesus.
Our Lord; (Phil. 2:9–11)	No nation, no king, no Caesar comes first: only Jesus is Lord. He has all authority and power; only he deserves praise and worship.
Who was conceived by the Holy Spirit, and born of the Virgin Mary; (Luke 1:35)	Jesus' birth and life were a miracle. By being fully human, Jesus has given us an example of life, taken upon himself the penalty of sin, and given us a new life and a new future.
Suffered under Pontius Pilate, (Luke 23:23–25)	Many have blamed Jews for Jesus' death. The Creed makes it clear that Pilate decided Jesus' death. Jesus died an innocent man. Pilate's injustice contrasts with God's justice; Pilate's arrogance contrasts with Jesus' humility.
Was crucified, died, and buried (1 Cor. 15:3–4)	These events really happened. Jesus' crucifixion and death were not merely staged; Jesus' death was real and a sad necessity for our sake.
He descended into hell; (1 Peter 3:18–19)	The meaning of this line is not clear; some think it refers to 1 Peter 3:19: "He went and preached to the spirits in prison." It is also possible to translate this line as "he descended to the dead," emphasizing the reality of Jesus' death. The phrase was not in the oldest available copy of the creed.
On the third day he rose from the dead; (1 Cor. 15:4)	Jesus' resurrection is fundamental. His resurrection points to the fulfillment of all justice and the hope for all believers. Jesus is the "firstborn from among the dead" (Col. 1:18).
He ascended into heaven and is seated at the right hand of the Father; (Luke 24:51)	Ascending to heaven and sitting at the right hand of the Father demonstrate Jesus' authority over the whole creation.
From thence he will come to judge the living and the dead. (2 Tim. 4:1; John 5:22)	Jesus' second coming will not be like a humble lamb. He will return like a triumphant king and judge. With his authority, he will judge all of creation. Christians rest assured that there is "no condemnation for those who are in Christ Jesus" (Rom. 8:1).
I believe in the Holy Spirit, (John 15:26; 16:7–14)	Jesus promised to send us a comforter, guide, equipper, and advocate. The Holy Spirit is God's presence in our midst.
The holy catholic church, (Gal. 3:26–29)	God has called his people out of sin and death; it is a group separated (holy) and from the whole world and throughout all time (catholic, or universal). The church is a people bought with the precious blood of Jesus on the cross.
The communion of saints, (Heb. 10:25)	In Jesus, all believers from all places and all times are brothers and sisters; we all share the same fellowship, the same Spirit, and the same Lord. We, who were many, are now one people in Jesus.
The forgiveness of sins, (Heb. 8:12; Luke 7:48)	Sin had broken our relationship with God, with creation, and with one another. Jesus has reconciled us with God, freeing us from our sin and death.
The resurrection of the body, and the life everlasting. (1 Thess. 4:16; John 10:28)	Unlike the Gnostics who viewed every physical reality as evil, Christians believe that they will receive new bodies and a new creation. Jesus' resurrected body was real (he could eat and could be touched); our resurrection bodies will also have a physical nature. And we will live with Jesus forever in a new creation.

HERESIES IN THE EARLY CHURCH

HERESY	SUMMARY	COMMENTS
DOCETISM First Century	This heresy denies the reality of Jesus' human nature. Jesus only *appeared* to be human. (The word *docetism* is derived from a Greek word meaning "appearance.") Docetism was imported directly from Gnosticism into Christianity.	Today many people deny Jesus' divinity and consider him *just* a human. But Christians who focus only on Jesus' divinity and ignore the physical reality of Jesus' resurrection fall into a mild form of docetism.
EBIONITISM First Century	Ebionites denied Jesus' divinity and proposed the full continuity of the Old Testament Law. In other words, Christians should still submit to the Old Testament Law. Ebionites rejected Paul's teachings.	This heresy is significant because it prompted the church to define itself as distinct from Judaism, though still connected to the Old Testament.
ADOPTIONISM Second Century	Adoptionism claims that Jesus was born as (only) a human. Later, he became divine when God *adopted* him. This common position among Gnostics is a form of *Monarchianism*.	The Bible clearly shows that Jesus *is* God. Adoptionism arises from a misplaced respect for God's uniqueness. The idea that God became human is very difficult to understand. Today, some scholars still teach adoptionism as a way to understand Jesus as a human being who became divine in a *metaphorical* way.
MANICHEANISM Second Century	A heresy fusing Christian, Zoroastrian and Buddhist beliefs in a religion that was very popular and widespread until around the AD 600's. Mani called himself the *Paraclete* who would complete the work of people like Zoroaster, Plato, Buddha, and Jesus.	Manicheanism is important because it spread Gnosticism in the West and in Christianity (Augustine was a Manichean before becoming a Christian). Mani did not believe in a personal God; good and evil were equal but opposing forces.
MARCIONISM Second Century	Marcion made a radical break between Christianity and the Old Testament. Marcion proclaimed himself a follower of Jesus but rejected Paul's writings and anything that sounded like the Old Testament.	Today, many Christians who ignore the Old Testament are functional Marcionites. Whatever our doctrinal differences may be, the church confesses that the whole Bible, both Old and New Testaments, is the Word of God.
MODALISM Second Century	Modalism teaches that God takes on different modes of being at different times. In the Old testament God manifested himself as the Father. In the New Testament, God manifested himself as the Son. In the Church age, God manifests himself as the Holy Spirit.	Modalism attempts to make sense of the difficult doctrine of the Trinity. However, it is inconsistent with biblical testimony. Some people today continue to hold to a form of modalism. Though they identify themselves as Christians, they understand God in modalist terms.

HERESY	SUMMARY	COMMENTS
MONTANISM Second/Third Century	Montanists emphasized the spiritual gift of prophecy. Montanus, the founder, believed he received direct revelation from God through the Holy Spirit. Church fathers were divided concerning his teachings. However, Montanus's followers were more radical, claiming their prophecies were superior to the Bible. They also identified their three leaders with the Father, the Son, and the Holy Spirit. The church condemned their teachings and their legalistic way of life.	This heresy reminds us of the importance of the Holy Spirit. It also warns us of the excesses of some prophetic claims. Some Christians believe the Holy Spirit continues to give the gift of prophecy in our times. However, such prophecy must depend on biblical revelation to be valid.
APOLLINARIANISM Fourth Century	The idea that Jesus had a full human body and soul, but no human reason. Instead, the divine *logos* was Jesus' rationality. Apollinaris, Bishop of Laodicea, could not understand the union of two very different natures, human and divine. He attempted to preserve the divine glory by separating the human and the divine.	This view is based on a semi-Gnostic understanding of reality: the "soul" is good; the "material world" is bad. A rejection of the world as God's good creation can lead one to this position.
ARIANISM Fourth Century	Arianism argues that Jesus does not share the same *essence* with God, and thus does not share in the same divine nature with eternity and authority. The Nicene, Chalcedonian, and Athanasian Creeds are primarily responses to this heresy.	This heresy prompted the church to define its understanding of Christ. The question of Jesus' nature, divine or not, is directly related to his work of salvation.
MACEDONIANISM Fourth Century	A heresy similar to Arianism, also denying that Jesus is the same essence of God the Father, although affirming Jesus as eternal. In addition, believers denied the divinity of the Holy Spirit.	Despite the strong condemnation from the Nicaea Council, the rise of this heresy shows the extension and powerful effect of the Arian heresy in Christianity. It extended the doubts from the nature of Jesus to the nature of the Holy Spirit.
PELAGIANISM Fourth Century	Pelagius taught that sin had not affected human nature at all. Adam's sin set a "bad example," which people choose to follow or not. Christ came to offer a "good example" of life. Salvation means choosing to follow Jesus' example.	Pelagianism represents a conscious rejection of God's grace-filled action to save humans and reconcile people with himself. A milder form, called semi-Pelagianism, suggests that we cooperate with God for our justification.
NESTORIANISM Fifth Century	Nestorius attempted to explain Jesus' incarnation by suggesting that Jesus has two separate natures: a human and a divine nature. However, the separation is so extreme that it would appear that Jesus had both two natures and two persons: a divine nature for one "person" and a human one for another "person."	Nestorianism was a reaction to the teaching that Jesus had only one nature (Apollinarianism is an example of this teaching). This teaching caused a great split in Christianity.

THE NICENE CREED

The greatest doctrinal challenge to the church arose internally. Arius, a priest in Alexandria, suggested that if God begat Jesus, then Jesus had an origin. As such, Jesus did not share in the same divine essence with the Father. Therefore, Jesus was a lesser god.

In AD 325, Constantine called the leaders of the church to participate in a council—that is, an assembly of bishops. They met in the city of Nicaea, in present-day Turkey. The Council of Nicaea, made up of about 300 participants, overwhelmingly voted against the Arian teachings—ancient documents suggest that only three bishops refused to sign their agreement. The council expressed its views about God, Jesus, and the church in the Nicene Creed.

NICENE CREED	MEANING	
We believe in one God, the Father Almighty, Maker *of heaven and earth, and* of all things visible and invisible.	As in the Apostles' Creed, the foundation of the Christian faith is the uniqueness of God. He alone is God. The Father is a distinct person, or individual reality, within the Godhead. In addition, God created *all* things. He is not created, but the Creator.	
And in one Lord Jesus Christ, *the only-begotten* Son of God, begotten of the Father *before all worlds*, Light of Light, very God of very God, begotten, not made, being of one substance with the Father; by whom all things were made;	The creed affirms Jesus' • Lordship: The same title applied to God the Father in the Old Testament. • Equality: Jesus is as much God as the Father. They share the same divine *essence*. Thus, Jesus is eternal. • Distinctness: Although they share the same essence, Jesus is a *person* distinct from the Father.	
Who for us, and for our salvation, came down *from heaven*, and was incarnate *by the Holy Ghost of the Virgin Mary*, and was made man; *he was crucified for us under Pontius Pilate,* and suffered, *and was buried,* and the third day he rose again, *according to the Scriptures,* and ascended into heaven, *and sits on the right hand of the Father*; from thence he shall come again, *with glory*, to judge the living and the dead; *whose kingdom shall have no end.*	The creed emphasizes both Jesus' divinity and humanity. • The image of coming down from heaven shows his divinity. • His miraculous virgin birth shows his humanity. • His suffering and death on the cross, again, show his full humanity. • His resurrection and ascension show his perfect work of salvation on behalf of humanity. • His final judgment shows his authority over the whole creation.	
And in the Holy Spirit, *the Lord and Giver of life, who proceeds from the Father, who with the Father and the Son together is worshiped and glorified, who spoke by the prophets.*	The creed confirms the Bible's doctrine of the Trinity: The Holy Spirit is fully divine, of the same *essence* as the Father and the Son, and is a distinct person within the Godhead. In the sixth century, Western churches added "who proceeds from the Father *and the Son*." It is this last addition, known as the *filioque* (Latin for "and the Son") that has caused division and conflict between the Eastern Orthodox and Western churches.	
In one holy catholic and apostolic church; we acknowledge one baptism for the remission of sins; we look for the resurrection of the dead, and the life of the world to come. Amen. *[NOTE: The words in cursive were added after the First Council of Nicaea in AD 325. The Council of Constantinople made these additions in AD 381.]*	One of the main purposes of the creed was to promote the unity of all believers in one universal church within the Apostolic tradition. Baptism represents this unity, as does the forgiveness of sins, the resurrection, and the world to come. These are all promises and hopes that link all Christians everywhere and at every time.	

A CHRISTIAN EMPIRE In AD 313, Constantine became the sole ruler of the Roman Empire. His Edict of Milan, put into effect in 313, granted full tolerance to all religions of the Empire. Constantine fought hard to gain stability for the Empire. Scholars have debated much whether Constantine really converted to Christianity—and if so, at what age he did. Whatever the case, Constantine became the protector and, in time, promoter of Christianity throughout the Empire.

During Constantine's reign, the Arian controversy threatened to divide Christianity and bring chaos to the Empire. Constantine understood that a divided Christianity would also divide the Empire. To keep his Empire together, he needed to keep Christianity together. From a political standpoint, the Nicaea Council solved and prevented a schism in Christianity and the Roman Empire.

COMMENTS

In Gnosticism, the God of the Bible is just the *demiurge*, an evil god who brought about the material world. This god is himself created.

In the New Testament, Jesus' Lordship is directly connected to his divinity. He is not Lord simply because he earned it; rather, he is Lord because he is God. Arius tried to understand the Incarnation, but his approach ignores the broad context of the Scriptures.

Heresies about Jesus denied either his full divinity or his full humanity.
- Denying Jesus' divinity removes his ability to save humanity from sin and death. Jesus is reduced to being a *model* of perfection.
- Denying Jesus' humanity removes his ability to intercede and represent humanity in his death.

The natural consequence of denying Jesus' divinity is that the Holy Spirit is not divine either. After the creed of AD 325, the heresy about the Holy Spirit arose as a follow-up to Arianism.

The Arian controversy threatened to split the young and growing church. The creed allows the possibility of unity of belief and practice. The word *catholic* means "universal," in the sense of the whole world. It refers, then, to the worldwide fellowship of all believers.

ATHANASIUS AND THE TRINITY

Athanasius was one of the most active opponents of Arius' teachings. His persistence and clear mind helped the church to clarify its positions and write it in a creed, the Nicene Creed.

Athanasius' teachings are summarized in the Athanasian Creed. While it is likely that Athanasius did not write it, the creed contains his teachings and main ideas. The Athanasian Creed begins by affirming, "This is what the catholic [or universal] faith teaches: we worship one God in the Trinity and the Trinity in unity. We distinguish among the persons, but we do not divide the substance [or essence]." After unpacking these ideas, the creed concludes, "So that in all things, as aforesaid, the Unity in Trinity and the Trinity in Unity is to be worshipped."

THE CHALCEDONIAN CREED

Map of Constantinopolis (Istanbul), printed in 1572 © Nikolay Staykov

Understanding the incarnation of Jesus—the embodiment of God the Son in human flesh—was one of the greatest challenges for the early church. In AD 451 the Council of Chalcedon (located in today's Turkey) provided a clear statement of the Apostolic teachings concerning Jesus. The Chalcedonian Creed made it clear that Jesus is fully God and fully human, two natures existing in perfect harmony in one person.

HERESIES TODAY

Many heresies—wrong beliefs—relate to two central biblical teachings: the Trinity and the Incarnation. Misunderstanding who God is will lead to misunderstanding what God has done and will do. Knowing the basic teachings of the church will help us identify and respond to heresies still existing today. The following chart provides some basic points to keep in mind about how ancient heresies show up today and what the correct, biblical teachings are.

ANCIENT HERESY	WHAT IT LOOKS LIKE TODAY	
GNOSTICISM	• Confusing God with his creation. Taking things and people as part of the divine. • Rejecting the physical world as evil. • Belief that salvation is inside every person. • Speaking about Jesus as a guru or only as a great teacher. • "Pop spirituality" based on Gnostic ideas. *The Secret*, *The Power of Now*, and many self-help teachings fall into this category.	
MARCIONISM	• Rejecting the Old Testament. • Rejecting anything that sounds too Jewish from the New Testament. • Completely divorcing the Old Testament from the New Testament.	
MONARCHIANISM	• Denying the Trinity. • Claiming one god with three functions: First appearing as Father, then as Son, and now as Holy Spirit. • Both forms are active: Adoptionism and Modalism.	
ARIANISM APOLLINARIANISM DOCETISM MACEDONIANISM NESTORIANISM	• Claims that Jesus was human only and became divine. • Claims that Jesus was only divine and merely appeared human. • Claims that Jesus was two persons with two natures in one being.	
MONTANISM	• Offering prophecy beyond what the Bible reveals. • Claiming greater authority than the Bible. • Making the Holy Spirit more important than Jesus. • Using prophetic gifts to abuse other Christians' trust and faith. • Misleading people through unverifiable prophecies.	

HERESIES ABOUT CHRIST CORRECTED IN THE CHALCEDONIAN CREED

SUBJECT	HERETICAL POSITION	APOSTOLIC TEACHING
Nature of Christ	Arianism: Jesus was the first created being, similar to God, but not fully divine like the Father. Docetism: Jesus was only a divine being. He merely *appeared* human.	Christ is *fully* God and *fully* human.
Relationship of Christ's Two Natures	Nestorianism: No connection between Jesus' two natures. Practically, Jesus had two natures and was two persons. Eutychianism: The divine and human natures are fused into one nature.	Two natures, divine and human, and one person.

CORRECT APOSTOLIC TEACHING	COMMENTS
• God is the Creator of all things. • The world is good, though corrupted through human sin. • Salvation is possible only through Jesus.	• Christians need to be careful not to reject this material world. Radical separation of the body and soul is not a biblical teaching. God loves the world he made. He blessed it. We should do likewise.
• The Old and New Testaments together are the Word of God. • Some ideas and concepts in the Old Testament continued in the New. Others Jesus fulfilled and are no longer binding in the New Testament. • God reveals himself in both Testaments. But Jesus is the fullness of God's revelation to humanity.	• Sometimes Christians make too strong a distinction between the Law and the Gospel. • The New Testament revelation is more complete than the Old Testament revelation because of Jesus (Heb. 1:1–3). • The revelation of the New Testament depends on God's works and words in the Old Testament.
• There is one God in three distinct Persons: God the Father, the Son, and the Holy Spirit. • All three persons participate in the divine nature but have distinct personalities. • All three are involved in God's work of Creation, redemption, and restoration.	• Some groups believe that only Jesus (of the three members of the Trinity) is God. This is a form of modalism. • Other groups, like the Jehovah's Witnesses, confess a form of adoptionism. They deny that Jesus is fully God. Rather, they may believe Jesus is an angel, a special divine being, but not God.
• Jesus is the second Person of the Trinity. • He is fully God and fully human. • He is one person with two natures, divine and human. The natures are joined, but not mixed.	• Jehovah's Witnesses and Mormons show clear examples of such errors. • It is possible to emphasize Jesus' divine character to the point of forgetting that he is fully human as well. Jesus suffered, was hungry, and was tempted like any other human.
• God has revealed his will in the Scriptures and in Jesus. • The Holy Spirit only testifies about Jesus. • Although there are gifts of prophecy, prophecies are still subject to the authority of the Bible. • Prophecies from God are for building up the church, not for personal gain.	• Most founders of current cults—like Jehovah's Witnesses, Mormonism, and Christian Science—have claimed to receive new revelations from God. • These revelations contradict the Bible. • The prophetic claims of groups like Heaven's Gate, Peoples Temple, and many others have had tragic consequences.

WHY DO THE CREEDS MATTER?

1. *Creeds help Christians to distinguish between essential and nonessential beliefs.* Not everyone who disagrees with you is a heretic! There are some beliefs on which Christians cannot compromise. On others, we can agree to disagree. The creeds—which focus on the essential beliefs that cannot be compromised—help us to distinguish between essential and nonessential beliefs.

2. *Creeds help Christians to focus their faith and worship on the issues that matter most.* The issues that the creeds emphasize—such as the Trinity, the character of God, the nature of Jesus, and the resurrection, for example—are the ones that the earliest Christians understood to matter most. These same beliefs can provide a unifying focus for contemporary Christians' teaching and worship.

3. *Creeds help Christians to articulate clearly how their beliefs differ from other teachings.* The apostle Peter commanded his readers always "to be ready to provide to anyone who asks a defense for the hope that is in you" (1 Peter 3:15-16). When it comes to giving a defense for our faith, the creeds are crucial! When someone asks what Christians believe about the resurrection of Jesus, the Apostles' and Nicene Creeds provide concise summaries of this core doctrine. When a child in Sunday school asks why Jesus came to earth, a teacher who remembers the Nicene Creed can tell the child immediately, "It was for us and for our salvation." If someone asks whether the virgin conception of Jesus really matters, the Christian who knows the creeds can immediately recall that, even for the earliest believers in Jesus, this was an essential doctrine.

Author: Benjamin Galan, MTS, ThM, Adjunct Professor of OT Hebrew and Literature at Fuller Seminary.
Special thanks to Timothy Paul Jones, PhD, Southern Baptist Theological Seminary in Louisville, Kentucky; and Paul Carden, Executive Director, Centers for Apologetics Research (CFAR).

Note: The text of the Apostles' Creed and the Nicene Creed were modified from *Creeds of Christendom, Vol. 1* by Philip Schaff.

The Trinity

What Is the Trinity?

Answers to Misunderstandings

What Early Christians Said about the Trinity

What Is the Trinity?

What Christians Believe About the Trinity

In the simplest of terms, Christians believe:

There is only one God, and this one God exists as one essence in three Persons.

The three Persons are   God the Father
God the Son (Jesus Christ)
God the Holy Spirit (also called the Holy Ghost)

Early Christians used this diagram to explain the Trinity. The Father, Son, and Holy Spirit are all God, but they are not three names for the same Person.

The Persons are distinct: The Father is not the Son.
The Son is not the Holy Spirit.
The Holy Spirit is not the Father.

The Trinity and the Bible

God is one absolutely perfect divine Being in three Persons. His *being* is what God *is*, in relation to the universe he created. The three are called Persons because they relate to one another in personal ways.

When Christians talk about believing in one God in three Persons (the Trinity), they do NOT mean:

> 1 God in 3 Gods, or
> 3 Persons in 1 Person, or
> 3 Persons in 3 Gods, or
> 1 Person in 3 Gods

Rather, they mean:

> 1 God in 3 Persons

Therefore,

The Father is God—the first Person
> of the Trinity.

The Son is God—the second Person
> of the Trinity.

The Holy Spirit is God—the third Person
> of the Trinity. (The title "Holy Ghost" is an older English expression for "Holy Spirit." Each is an acceptable translation of the phrase in the Bible.)

Theophilus, sixth bishop of Antioch, Syria, is the first person known to have used the word "Trinity" in his work, *Refutation of Autolycus* (AD 168)

Why do Christians Believe in the Trinity?

The Bible clearly teaches that there is only one God, yet all three Persons are called God.

There is only one God:

- *"Hear, O Israel: The LORD our God is one LORD."*—Deuteronomy 6:4
- *"Before me there was no God formed, neither shall there be after me."*—Isaiah 43:10

The Father is God:

- *"Grace be unto you, and peace, from God our Father and from the Lord Jesus Christ."*—1 Corinthians 1:3 (Also 1 Corinthians 8:6; Ephesians 4:4–6.)

The Son is God:

- *"The Word was God."*—John 1:1b (Also John1:1-5, 14.) Jesus is identified as "the Word."
- *"I and the Father are one."*—John 10:30 (Also John 10:32–33.)
- Jesus' disciple Thomas addressed Jesus as *"My Lord and my God"* (John 20:28).

    Jesus did not tell Thomas he was mistaken; Instead Jesus accepted these titles. Other people in Scripture, notably Paul and Barnabas (Acts 14), refused to accept worship as gods.

The Trinity and the Bible

- *"But unto the Son he saith, Thy throne, O God, is for ever and ever: a sceptre of righteousness is the sceptre of thy kingdom."*—*Hebrews 1:6-8*
- *"Wherefore God also hath highly exalted him, and given him a name which is above every name: That at the name of Jesus every knee should bow, of things in heaven, and things in earth, and things under the earth; and that every tongue should confess that Jesus Christ is Lord, to the glory of God the Father."*—*Philippians 2:9–11*

  Paul, the writer of Philippians, is saying about Jesus what Isaiah 45:23 says about the LORD, and then Paul concludes that Jesus is LORD, that is, the same LORD God of the Old Testament.

See these passages about Jesus' deity: Isaiah 7:14; 9:6; John 1:1–18; 8:58–59; 10:30; Acts 20:28; Romans 9:5; 10:9–13; Colossians 1:15–16; 2:9; Titus 2:13; Hebrews 1:3, 8; 2 Peter 1:1; 1 John 5:20.

The Holy Spirit is God:

- *"But Peter said, Ananias, why hath Satan filled thine heart to lie to the Holy Ghost?... Thou hast not lied unto men, but unto God."*—*Acts 5:3–4*

This verse equates the Holy Spirit (Holy Ghost) with God.

- *"Now the Lord is that Spirit."*—*2 Corinthians 3:17*

  "The Lord" here refers to "the LORD" in the Old Testament verse (Exodus 34:34) Paul had just quoted in the previous verse (2 Corinthians 3:16).

More than 60 Bible passages mention the three Persons together:

- Matthew 3:16–17 "And Jesus, when he was baptized, went up straightway out of the water: and, lo, the heavens were opened unto him, and he saw the Spirit of God descending like a dove, and lighting upon him: And lo a voice from heaven, saying, This is my beloved Son, in whom I am well pleased."
- Matthew 28:19 "Go ye therefore, and teach all nations, baptizing them in the name of the Father, and of the Son, and of the Holy Ghost."
- 2 Corinthians 13:14 "The grace of the Lord Jesus Christ, and the love of God, and the communion of the Holy Ghost, be with you all."
- Ephesians 4:4–6 "There is one body, and one Spirit, even as ye are called in one hope of your calling; one Lord, one faith, one baptism, one God and Father of all, who is above all, and through all, and in you all."
- Titus 3:4–6 "But after that the kindness and love of God our Saviour toward man appeared, not by works of righteousness which we have done, but according to his mercy he saved us, by the washing of regeneration, and renewing of the Holy Ghost; which he shed on us abundantly through Jesus Christ our Saviour."

See also John 3:34–35; 14:26; 15:26; 16:13–15; Romans 14:17–18; 15:13–17; 15:30; 1 Corinthians 6:11, 17–19; 12:4–6; 2 Corinthians 1:21–22; 3:4–6; Galatians 2:21–3:2; 4:6; Ephesians 2:18; 3:11–17; 5:18–20; Colossians 1:6–8; 1 Thessalonians 1:1–5; 4:2–8; 5:18–19; 2 Thessalonians 3:5; Hebrews 9:14; 1 Peter 1:2; 1 John 3:23–24; 4:13–14; Jude 20–21.

Misunderstandings About the Trinity

Misunderstanding #1: "The word 'Trinity' does not appear in the Bible; it is a belief made up by Christians in the 4th century."

Truth: It is true that the word "Trinity" does not appear in the Bible, but the Trinity is nevertheless a Bible-based belief. The word "incarnation" does not appear in the Bible either, but we use it as a one-word summary of our belief that Jesus was God in the flesh.

The word "Trinity" was used to explain the eternal relationship between the Father, the Son, and the Holy Spirit. Many Bible passages express the Trinity. False beliefs flourished during the early days of Christianity, and still do. Early Christians constantly defended their beliefs. The following early church leaders and/or writings all defended the doctrine of the Trinity long before AD 300:

Approximate Dates:

AD 96	**Clement**, the third bishop of Rome
AD 90-100	**The Teachings of the Twelve Apostles**, the "Didache"
AD 90?	**Ignatius**, bishop of Antioch
AD 155	**Justin Martyr**, great Christian writer
AD 168	**Theophilus**, the sixth bishop of Antioch
AD 177	**Athenagoras**, theologian
AD 180	**Irenaeus**, bishop of Lyons
AD 197	**Tertullian**, early church leader
AD 264	**Gregory Thaumaturgus**, early church leader

Misunderstanding #2: "Christians believe there are three Gods."

Truth: Christians believe in only one God.

Some people might believe that Christians are polytheists (people who believe in many gods) because Christians refer to the Father as God, the Son as God, and the Holy Spirit as God. But Christians believe in only one God. The Bible says there is only one God. But it also calls three distinct Persons "God." Over the centuries people have tried to come up with simple explanations for the Trinity. There are limits to every illustration, but some are helpful. For example, it has been said that

God is not	$1 + 1 + 1 = 3$
God is	$1 \times 1 \times 1 = 1$

The Trinity is a profound doctrine that must be accepted by faith. Accepting a doctrine by faith does not exclude reason, but it also means that we cannot always apply the same logic that we use in mathematics. Without the Trinity, the Christian doctrine of salvation cannot stand. Some religious groups that claim to believe in the God of the Bible, but reject the Trinity, have an understanding of salvation that is based on good works.

St. Patrick is believed to have used the shamrock as a way of illustrating the Trinity. He asked, "Is this one leaf or three? If one leaf, why are there three lobes of equal size? If three leaves, why is there just one stem? If you cannot explain so simple a mystery as the shamrock, how can you hope to understand one so profound as the Holy Trinity?" Even though this is an overly simple way to explain the Trinity, some teachers find it helpful.

St. Patrick (AD 432) used the shamrock to illustrate the Trinity.

Misunderstandings About the Trinity

Misunderstanding #3: "Jesus is not God."

Truth: Jesus is God, the Second Person of the Trinity.

1. Jesus' own claims

- **He forgave sin.** We may forgive sins committed against us, but we cannot forgive sins committed against others. Jesus has the authority to forgive any sin (Mark 2:5–12; Luke 5:21).
- **He accepted worship as God and claimed to deserve the same honor as the Father** (Matthew 14:33; 28:17–18; John 5:22–23; 9:38; 17:5).
- **He claimed to be the divine Son of God,** a title the Jews rightly understood to be a claim to equality with God (John 5:17–18; 10:30–33; 19:7).

2.

Traits Unique to God	Traits of Jesus
Creation is "the work of his hands"—alone (Genesis 1:1; Psalm 102:25; Isaiah 44:24)	Creation is "the work of his hands" —all things created in and through him (John 1:3; Colossians 1:16; Hebrews 1:2, 10)
"The first and the last" (Isaiah 44:6)	"The first and the last" (Revelation 1:17; 22:13)
"Lord of lords" (Deuteronomy 10:17; Psalm 136:3)	"Lord of lords" (1 Timothy 6:15; Revelation 17:14; 19:16)
Unchanging and eternal (Psalm 90:2; 102:26–27; Malachi 3:6)	Unchanging and eternal (John 8:58; Colossians 1:17; Hebrews 1:11–12; 13:8)
Judge of all people (Genesis 18:25; Psalms 94:2; 96:13; 98:9)	Judge of all people (John 5:22; Acts 17:31; 2 Cor. 5:10; 2 Timothy 4:1)
Only Savior; no other God can save (Isaiah 43:11; 45:21–22; Hosea 13:4)	Savior of the world; no salvation apart from him (John 4:42; Acts 4:12; Titus 2:13; 1 John 4:14)
Redeems from their sins a people for his own possession (Exodus 19:5; Psalm 130:7–8; Ezekiel 37:23)	Redeems from their sins a people for his own possession (Titus 2:14)
Hears and answers prayers of those who call on him (Psalm 86:5–8; Isaiah 55:6–7; Jer. 33:3; Joel 2:32)	Hears and answers prayers of those who call on him (John 14:14; Romans 10:12–13; 1 Corinthians 1:2; 2 Corinthians 12:8–9)
Only God has divine glory (Isaiah 42:8; 48:11)	Jesus has divine glory (John 17:5)
Worshiped by angels (Psalm 97:7)	Worshiped by angels (Hebrews 1:6)

Misunderstandings About the Trinity

Misunderstanding #4: "Jesus is a *lesser* God than the Father."

Truth: Jesus is co-equal with God the Father. People who deny this truth may use the following arguments and verses. (These heresies date back to Arius, AD 319.)

Verses wrongly used to teach that Christ was created:

1. Colossians 1:15: If Christ is "the firstborn of all creation," was he created?

Answer: "Firstborn" cannot mean that Christ was created, because Paul says that all of creation was made in and for Christ, and that he exists before all creation and holds it together (Colossians 1:16–17). The "firstborn" traditionally was the main heir. In context Paul is saying that Christ, as God's Son, is the main heir of all creation (verses 12–14).

2. John 3:16: Does "only begotten Son" mean Jesus had a beginning?

Answer: "Only-begotten" does not mean that Jesus had a beginning; it means that Jesus is God's "unique" Son. In Hebrews 11:17, Isaac is called Abraham's "unique" son, even though Abraham had other children (Genesis 22:2; 25:1-6). Jesus is God's unique Son because only Jesus is fully God and eternally the Father's Son (John 1:1-3, 14–18).

3. Proverbs 8:22: Does this mean that Christ ("Wisdom") was "created"?

Answer: This is not a literal description of Christ; it is a personification of wisdom. For example, Christ did not dwell in heaven with someone named Prudence (8:12); he did not build a house with seven pillars (9:1). This verse says in a poetic way that God used wisdom in creating the world (3:19–20).

Verses wrongly used to teach that Jesus is inferior to the Father:

1. John 14:28: If "the Father is greater than" Jesus, how can Jesus be God?

Answer: In his human life on earth Jesus voluntarily shared our natural limitations in order to save us. After he rose from the dead, Jesus returned to the glory he had with the Father (John 17:5; Philippians 2:9–11). In that restored glory, Jesus was able to send the Holy Spirit and empower his disciples to do even greater works than Jesus did while he was here in the flesh (John 14:12, 26–28).

2. 1 Corinthians 15:28: If Jesus is God, why will he be subject to the Father?

Answer: Jesus humbly and voluntarily submits himself to the Father's will for a time (Philippians 2:5–11). But, as the pre-existent and eternal Son, he is co-equal with God the Father.

3. Mark 13:32: If Jesus is God, how could he not know when he would return?

Answer: Jesus voluntarily lowered himself to experience the limitations of human life. Paradoxically, while Jesus continued to be God, he chose to limit his access to knowledge (John 16:30). Paradoxes like this (not contradictions) are exactly what we would expect if, as the Bible says, God chose to live as a real human being (John 1:1, 14).

Misunderstandings About the Trinity

Misunderstanding #5: "The Father, the Son, and the Spirit are just different titles for Jesus, or three different ways that God has revealed himself."

Truth: The Bible clearly shows that the Father, Son, and Holy Spirit are distinct persons.

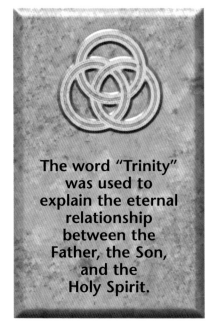

Some people think that the doctrine of the Trinity contradicts the truth that there is only one God. They argue that Jesus alone is the one true God, and therefore that Jesus is "the name of the Father and the Son and the Holy Spirit" (Matthew 28:19), and not just the name of the Son. While it is certainly true that there is only one God, we must allow the Bible to define what this means. And the Bible makes it quite clear that the Father, Son, and Holy Spirit are distinct persons:

The word "Trinity" was used to explain the eternal relationship between the Father, the Son, and the Holy Spirit.

- The Father sends the Son (1 John 4:14; Galatians 4:4).
- The Father sends the Spirit (John 14:26; Galatians 4:6).
- The Son speaks, not on his own, but on behalf of the Father (John 8:28; 12:49).
- The Spirit speaks, not on his own, but on behalf of Jesus (John 16:13–15).
- The Father loves the Son, and the Son loves the Father (John 3:35; 5:20; 14:31).
- The Father and the Son count as two witnesses (John 5:31–37; 8:16–18).
- The Father and the Son glorify one another (John 17:1–5), and the Spirit glorifies Jesus the Son (John 16:14).
- The Son is an Advocate for us with the Father (1 John 2:1; Greek, *parakletos*); Jesus the Son sent the Holy Spirit, who is another Advocate (John 14:16, 26).
- Jesus Christ is not the Father, but the Son of the Father (2 John 3).

In Matthew 28:19, Jesus is not identifying himself as the Father, Son, and Holy Spirit. He is saying that Christian baptism identifies a person as one who believes in the Father, in the Son whom the Father sent to die for our sins, and in the Holy Spirit whom the Father and the Son sent to dwell in our hearts.

Misunderstandings About the Trinity

Misunderstanding #6: "Jesus wasn't really fully God and fully man."

Throughout history many people have balked at the idea that Jesus is both fully God and fully man. They have tried to resolve this paradox by saying that Jesus was a mere man through whom God spoke, or that he was God and merely appeared to be human, or some other "simpler" belief. Admittedly the idea that in Jesus, God became a man, is difficult for us to comprehend. But the Incarnation—the truth that God became flesh—is the ultimate proof that nothing is too hard for God (Genesis 18:14; Luke 1:37). And this truth is clearly taught in the Bible.

The Bible clearly shows that Jesus was fully human:

As a child, he grew physically, intellectually, socially, and spiritually (Luke 2:40, 52).

He grew tired; he slept; he sweat; he was hungry and thirsty; he bled and died; his body was buried (Matthew 4:2; 8:24; Luke 22:44; John 4:6–7; 19:28–42).

After he rose from the dead, he ate and drank with people and let them see his scars and touch his body (Luke 24:39–43; John 20:27–29; Acts 10:41).

The Bible also clearly shows that Jesus was fully God:

Jesus did on earth what only God can do: he commanded the forces of nature (Matthew 8:23–27; 14:22, 33); forgave sins (Mark 2:1–12); claimed to be superior to the Sabbath law (John 5:17–18); and gave life to whomever he pleased (John 5:19–23).

Paul said that God purchased the church with his own blood (Acts 20:28).

Paul also said that the rulers of this world unwittingly crucified the Lord of glory (1 Corinthians 2:8).

All the fullness of God's nature and being resides in Jesus' risen body (Colossians 2:9).

Irenaeus, early church leader (AD 177), writes, "Now the Church, . . . received from the apostles and their disciples its faith in one God, and the father Almighty, who made the heaven, and the earth, and the seas, and all that is in them, and in one Christ Jesus, the Son of God, who was made flesh for our salvation, and in the Holy Spirit, who through the prophets proclaimed the dispensations of God..."

Important Bible Verses and References

Divine Attributes	Father	Son	Holy Spirit
Eternal	Romans 16:26–27	Revelation 1:17	Hebrews 9:14
Creator of all things	Psalm 100:3	Colossians 1:16	Psalm 104:30
Omnipresent (capable of being all places at once)	Jeremiah 23:24	Ephesians 1:23	Psalm 139:7
Omniscient (knows all things)	1 John 3:20	John 21:17	1 Corinthians 2:10
Wills and acts supernaturally	Ephesians 1:5	Matthew 8:31	1 Corinthians 12:11
Gives life	Genesis 1:11–31 see also John 5:21	John 1:4 see also John 5:21	Romans 8:10–11 see also John 3:8
Strengthens believers	Psalm 138:3	Philippians 4:13	Ephesians 3:16

Books

Christ Before the Manger by Ron Rhodes (Grand Rapids: Baker, 1992). What the Bible says about Jesus before he became a man. Also see Rhodes's book *The Complete Book of Bible Answers.*

Creeds, Councils and Christ by Gerald Bray (Downers Grove, IL: InterVarsity Press, 1984). More advanced analysis of the origins and biblical basis of the creeds.

God in Three Persons by E. Calvin Beisner, (Wheaton: Tyndale House, 1984). Popular overview of the historical development of the doctrine.

Jesus, Divine Messiah: The New Testament Witness by Robert L. Reymond (Phillipsburg, NJ: Presbyterian & Reformed, 1990). Advanced biblical study, defending Christ's deity primarily against modern critical theories.

Oneness Pentecostals and the Trinity by Gregory A. Boyd (Grand Rapids: Baker, 1992). Biblical critique of the belief held by Oneness Pentecostals that Jesus is the Father, Son, and Holy Spirit.

The Trinity by Edward H. Bickersteth (Grand Rapids: Kregel, 1957). Classic exposition of the doctrine from a multitude of biblical texts.

Why You Should Believe in the Trinity by Robert M. Bowman, Jr. (Grand Rapids: Baker, 1989). Answers to various criticisms of the doctrine.

Internet

Watchman Fellowship www.watchman.org/subindex.htm
   Specializes in teaching biblical interpretation and in tracking numerous religious groups that deny the Trinity and other essential Christian doctrines (Scroll down to *Trinity* in this alphabetical list of topics.)

Blue Letter Bible www.blueletterbible.org/Comm/robert_bowman/trinity.html
   On-line interactive reference library continuously updated from the teachings and commentaries of selected pastors and teachers.

Apologetics Index www.apologeticsindex.org/t10.html

Institute for Religious Research www.irr.org/mit/trinity1.html

A simple illustration:

Ice, Water, Steam

All have the same nature, water.

(But of course, the Father, Son, and Holy Spirit are God at the *same* time.)

Scripture taken from the HOLY BIBLE: KING JAMES VERSION
Contributors: Robert M. Bowman, Jr.; Dennis L. Okholm, PhD; Gary M. Burge, PhD; Paul Carden; Robert Cubillos; Ron Rhodes, PhD

Life of Jesus

Why Did He Come?

What Did He Say?

Why Did He Die?

"Who do people say the Son of Man is?"

—Matthew 16:13

Jesus asked this question about himself to his disciples around 2,000 years ago. His disciples replied with answers based on things they knew or had experienced: "Some say John the Baptist; others say Elijah; and still others, Jeremiah or one of the prophets" (v. 14).

People in Jesus' day had expectations about who he was and arrived at their conclusions based on those expectations. Today it is not very different. People gather ideas about Jesus from many places: from television and movies, from books and newspapers, from family, school, and office conversations. Some of these ideas are right on the mark—others miss the mark entirely.

Some people say Jesus was just a popular preacher or a guru of ethical living. Others say it is not even important to know who Jesus is. But for people who have given their lives to Jesus and have experienced life in a new and wonderful way, the question about Jesus' identity is of greater-than-life importance.

After asking about what other people say, Jesus turned to his disciples and asked, "But what about you? Who do you say I am?" (v. 15). Peter answered, "You are the Christ, the Son of the living God" (v. 16).

What does it mean that Jesus is "the Christ" and "the Son"? It means that he is much more than a popular preacher, a prophet, or a wise teacher. Who is Jesus? The following pages will answer this fundamental question. To understand who Jesus is, it is important to understand what he taught, how he lived, what he said, and what those who knew him best said— those who knew him as "the Christ, the Son of the living God."

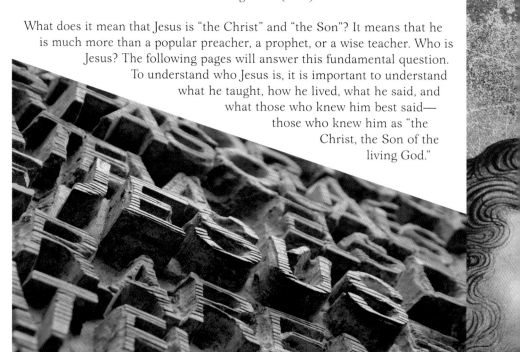

1. Who is Jesus?

WHAT JESUS SAID

"I am the way and the truth and the life. No one comes to the Father except through me."—John 14:6

"I am the bread of life. He who comes to me will never go hungry, and he who believes in me will never be thirsty... And this is the will of him who sent me, that I shall lose none of all that he has given me, but raise them up at the last day. For my Father's will is that everyone who looks to the Son and believes in him shall have eternal life, and I will raise him up at the last day."—John 6:35

"I am the light of the world. Whoever follows me will never walk in darkness, but will have the light of life.'"—John 8:12

See also Matthew 11:27–29; John 8:58; 10:30.

WHAT THOSE WHO KNEW HIM BEST SAID

"In the beginning was the Word, and the Word was with God, and the Word was God. He was with God in the beginning. Through him all things were made; without him nothing was made that has been made. In him was life, and that life was the light of men.... The Word became flesh and made his dwelling among us. We have seen his glory, the glory of the One and Only, who came from the Father, full of grace and truth.... From the fullness of his grace we have all received one blessing after another.
For the law was given through Moses; grace and truth came through Jesus Christ."—John 1:1–4, 14–17
John was one of Jesus' closest friends and earliest followers who was at the scene of Jesus' execution.

"For you know that it was not with perishable things such as silver or gold that you were redeemed from the empty way of life handed down to you from your forefathers, but with the precious blood of Christ, a lamb without blemish or defect. He was chosen before the creation of the world, but was revealed in these last times for your sake."—1 Peter 1:18–20
Peter, one of Jesus' twelve disciples, wrote this to Christians in the first century AD.

See also Matthew 16:16; Colossians 2:9; Hebrews 1:3.

WHAT GOD THE FATHER SAID

"While [Peter] was still speaking, a bright cloud enveloped them, and a voice from the cloud said, 'This is my Son, whom I love; with him I am well pleased. Listen to him!'"—Matthew 17:5
God the Father spoke plainly about Jesus.

WHAT NATURE SAID

"Jesus was in the stern, sleeping on a cushion. The disciples woke him and said to him, 'Teacher, don't you care if we drown?' He got up, rebuked the wind and said to the waves, 'Quiet! Be still!' Then the wind died down and it was completely calm. He said to his disciples, 'Why are you so afraid? Do you still have no faith?' They were terrified and asked each other, 'Who is this? Even the wind and the waves obey him!'"—Mark 4:38–41

The natural world obeyed Jesus' commands because he is its Creator.

See also Matthew 14:13–33.

WHAT THE DEMONS SAID

"In the synagogue there was a man possessed by a demon, an evil spirit. He cried out at the top of his voice, 'Ha! What do you want with us, Jesus of Nazareth? Have you come to destroy us? I know who you are—the Holy One of God!'"—Luke 4:33–34

The spiritual world recognized Jesus and his power.

See also Matthew 8:29; Mark 5:6–7.

Christ in the Storm on the Sea of Galilee by Rembrandt

WHAT OTHERS HAVE SAID

"We may note in passing that He was never regarded as a mere moral teacher. He did not produce that effect on any of the people who actually met Him. He produced mainly three effects—Hatred—Terror—Adoration. There was no trace of people expressing mild approval."—C.S. Lewis, Oxford and Cambridge professor and former agnostic (1898–1963)

"I know men and I tell you that Jesus Christ is no mere man. Between him and every other person in the world there is no possible term of comparison."
—Napoleon Bonaparte, French Emperor (1769–1821)

"Why don't the names of Buddha, Mohammed, Confucius offend people? The reason is that these others didn't claim to be God, but Jesus did."—Josh McDowell, Christian Evangelist and Apologist

"He possessed neither wealth nor influence. His relatives were inconspicuous, and had neither training nor formal education. In infancy He startled a king; in childhood He puzzled doctors; in manhood He ruled the course of nature, walked upon the billows as if pavement, and hushed the sea to sleep. He healed the multitudes without medicine and made no charge for His service. The names of the past proud statesmen of Greece and Rome have come and gone. The names of the past scientists, philosophers, and theologians have come and gone; but the name of this Man abounds more and more. Though time has spread nineteen hundred years between the people of this generation and the scene of His crucifixion, yet He still lives, Herod could not destroy Him, and the grave could not hold Him."—from "The Incomparable Christ"

Summary: Jesus was more than human. In fact, he was human and divine at the same time—the Son of God. He is the Creator who entered his creation.

2. What was his message?

WHAT JESUS SAID ABOUT HIS GOOD NEWS (THE GOSPEL)

"The time has come.... The kingdom of God is near. Repent and believe the good news!"—Mark 1:15

"And this is the will of him who sent me, that I shall lose none of all that he has given me, but raise them up at the last day. For my Father's will is that everyone who looks to the Son and believes in him shall have eternal life, and I will raise him up at the last day."—John 6:39–40

See also Matthew 4:23–24, 5:1–7:29; Mark 4:1–34; Luke 15:1–31; John 10:1–18; 15:1–17.

WHAT THOSE WHO KNEW HIM BEST SAID

"We are witnesses of everything he did in the country of the Jews and in Jerusalem. They killed him by hanging him on a tree, but God raised him from the dead on the third day and caused him to be seen. He was not seen by all the people, but by witnesses whom God had already chosen—by us who ate and drank with him after he rose from the dead. He commanded us to preach to the people and to testify that he is the one whom God appointed as judge of the living and the dead. All the prophets testify about him that everyone who believes in him receives forgiveness of sins through his name."—Acts 10:39–43

Spoken by Peter, one of Jesus' best friends, who was hand-picked by Jesus to be a leader after Jesus' death and resurrection.

See also Acts 2:14–41; 3:11–26; 4:8–12; 5:29–32.

WHAT OTHERS HAVE SAID

"The real truth is that while He came to preach the gospel, His chief object in coming was that there might be a gospel to preach."
—R.W. Dale, Congregationalist minister (1829–1895)

"Jesus does not give recipes that show the way to God as other teachers of religion do, He is himself the way."—Karl Barth, Theologian (1886–1968)

"The Gospel that represents Jesus Christ, not as a system of truth to be received, into the mind, as I should receive a system of philosophy, or astronomy, but it represents Him as a real, living, mighty Savior, able to save me now."—Catherine Booth, Cofounder of the Salvation Army (1829–1890)

Summary: The center of Jesus' message was himself. He impacted the world like no other human in history. Everything he did was good, and the greatest good he accomplished was through his death and rising from the dead. The good news he came to announce was also what he came to accomplish.

3. Why did he come?

WHAT JESUS SAID

"For God did not send his Son into the world to condemn the world, but to save the world through him."—John 3:17

"I tell you the truth, I am the gate for the sheep. All who ever came before me were thieves and robbers, but the sheep did not listen to them. I am the gate; whoever enters through me will be saved.... I have come that they may have life, and have it to the full."—John 10:7–10

See also Matthew 5:17; Mark 2:17; 10:45; Luke 12:49–51; 19:10; John 7:28; 9:39; 12:46.

WHAT THOSE WHO KNEW HIM BEST SAID

"Christ Jesus came into the world to save sinners—of whom I am the worst."—1 Timothy 1:15

Written by the apostle Paul who was viciously anti-Christian until a life-changing encounter with the resurrected Jesus.

See also John 1:11–12; 1 John 3:8.

WHAT THE PROPHETS SAID

"Surely he took up our infirmities and carried our sorrows, yet we considered him stricken by God, smitten by him, and afflicted."—Isaiah 53:4

Spoken by Isaiah, a prophet who saw what the Messiah (the Christ) would do more than 700 years before Jesus was born.

See also Genesis 49:10; Malachi 3:1–4.

WHAT OTHERS HAVE SAID

"The essence of Jesus' ministry was to bring the divine power into all the realms of death and thereby to call into question the finality of death. Light in the darkness, the mocker of the grave, divine love in the most godforsaken places, Jesus throws off balance the whole world of the small soul."—Robert Barron, Professor of Systematic Theology, Mundelein Seminary

"Nineteen centuries have come and gone and today he is the centerpiece of the human race and the leader of the column of progress. I am far within the mark when I say that all the armies that ever marched, all the navies that ever were built; all the parliaments that ever sat and all the kings that ever reigned, put together, have not affected the life of man upon this earth as powerfully as has that one solitary life."
—Attributed to James Allen Francis, Doctor of Divinity (1864–1928)

Summary: Jesus came to save the world.

4. Why did he die?

WHAT JESUS SAID

"From that time on Jesus began to explain to his disciples that he must go to Jerusalem and suffer many things at the hands of the elders, chief priests and teachers of the law, and that he must be killed and on the third day be raised to life."—Matthew 16:21

"'Did not the Christ have to suffer these things and then enter his glory?' And beginning with Moses and all the Prophets, he explained to them what was said in all the Scriptures concerning himself."—Luke 24:25–27

The Flagellation of Our Lord Jesus Christ by William A. Bouguereau

WHAT THE FIRST CHRISTIANS SAID

"This righteousness from God comes through faith in Jesus Christ to all who believe. There is no difference, for all have sinned and fall short of the glory of God, and are justified freely by his grace through the redemption that came by Christ Jesus. God presented him as a sacrifice of atonement, through faith in his blood. He did this to demonstrate his justice, because in his forbearance he had left the sins committed beforehand unpunished—he did it to demonstrate his justice at the present time, so as to be just and the one who justifies those who have faith in Jesus."—Romans 3:21–26

Paul wrote this to Christians in Rome, approximately AD 56.

WHAT THE PROPHETS SAID

"And I will pour out on the house of David and the inhabitants of Jerusalem a spirit of grace and supplication. They will look on me, the one they have pierced, and they will mourn for him.... On that day a fountain will be opened to the house of David and the inhabitants of Jerusalem, to cleanse them from sin and impurity."—Zechariah 12:10; 13:1

Spoken by the prophet Zechariah, approximately 400 years before Jesus, foretelling what would happen to the Messiah, the Christ.

WHAT OTHERS HAVE SAID

"If Jesus Christ was who He claimed to be, and He did die on a Cross at a point of time in history, then, for all history past and all history future it is relevant because that is the very focal point for forgiveness and redemption."—Josh McDowell, Christian Evangelist and Apologist

"No man ever loved like Jesus. He taught the blind to see and the dumb to speak. He died on the cross to save us. He bore our sins. And now God says, 'Because He did, I can forgive you.'"—Billy Graham, Christian Evangelist and Author

Summary: The Messiah's death was predicted long before he walked the earth. As the Messiah (the Christ), Jesus willingly allowed himself be put to death on the cross. In this way, he was sacrificed for the sins of all people. By dying a criminal's death through a miscarriage of human justice, Jesus balanced the scales of God's justice for the debt owed by the human race. Because of this, all who trust in him can be forgiven and receive salvation.

5. What about the empty tomb?

WHAT JESUS SAID

"[Jesus] said to them, 'This is what I told you while I was still with you: Everything must be fulfilled that is written about me in the Law of Moses, the Prophets and the Psalms.' Then he opened their minds so they could understand the Scriptures. He told them, 'This is what is written: The Christ will suffer and rise from the dead on the third day, and repentance and forgiveness of sins will be preached in his name to all nations, beginning at Jerusalem. You are witnesses of these things.'"—Luke 24:44–48

"A week later [after the empty tomb was discovered] his disciples were in the house again, and Thomas was with them. Though the doors were locked, Jesus came and stood among them and said, 'Peace be with you!' Then he said to Thomas, 'Put your finger here; see my hands. Reach out your hand and put it into my side. Stop doubting and believe.' Thomas said to him, 'My Lord and my God!'"
—John 20:26–28

WHAT THE MESSENGERS AT JESUS' EMPTY TOMB SAID

"On the first day of the week, very early in the morning, the women took spices they had prepared and went to the tomb. They found the stone rolled away from the tomb but when they entered, they did not find the body of the Lord Jesus. While they were wondering about this, suddenly two men in clothes that gleamed like lightening stood beside them. In their fright the women bowed down with their faces to the ground, but the men said to them, 'Why do you look for the living among the dead? He is not here; he has risen!'"—Luke 24:1–6

The Resurrection by Carl Heinrich Bloch

Like these first messengers, the first Christians went on to boldly proclaim that Jesus had risen!

WHAT THE FIRST CHRISTIANS SAID

"For what I received I passed on to you as of first importance: that Christ died for our sins according to the Scriptures, that he was buried, that he was raised on the third day according to the Scriptures, and that he appeared to Peter, and then to the Twelve. After that, he appeared to more than five hundred of the brothers at the same time."—1 Corinthians 15:3–6

This was the testimony that the apostle Paul passed on to believers.

See also Matthew 28; Mark 16; John 20, 21; Acts 1:1–11; 2:22–36; 3:15–22; 1 Corinthians 15:3–8; Colossians 3:1; 1 Peter 3:18–22.

WHAT OTHERS HAVE SAID

"The Resurrection is the central theme in every Christian sermon reported in the Acts. The Resurrection, and its consequences were the 'gospel' or good news which the Christians brought."—C.S. Lewis, Oxford and Cambridge professor and former agnostic (1898–1963)

"Now there was about this time Jesus, a wise man, if it be lawful to call him a man; for he was a doer of wonderful works, a teacher of such men as receive the truth with pleasure. He drew over to him many Jews, and also many of the Greeks. This man was the Christ. And when Pilate had condemned him to the cross, upon his impeachment by the principal men among us, those who had loved him from the first did not forsake him, for he appeared to them alive on the third day, the divine prophets having spoken these and thousands of other wonderful things about him."—Josephus, Jewish historian (c. AD 37–100)

"[The Resurrection] is truly of great importance in Christianity; so great that His being or not being the Messiah stands or falls with it: so that these two important articles are inseparable and in effect make one. For since that time, believe one and you believe both; deny one of them, and you can believe neither."—John Locke, English philosopher (1632–1704)

"Confucius' tomb   –   occupied
Buddha's tomb   –   occupied
Mohammed's tomb –   occupied
Jesus' tomb   –   EMPTY."
—G.B. Hardy, Canadian scientist

© Tiffany Chan

Summary: There is no other adequate explanation for the empty tomb and the subsequent events than that Jesus rose up alive from the grave. He was seen by many people, and that many of those same people saw him rise up into heaven.

Time Line of the Life of Jesus

4 BC–AD 26

Jesus is born in Bethlehem. Luke 2:1–7

Jesus is presented in the temple. Luke 2:21–38

Mary and Joseph flee with their child Jesus to Egypt to escape King Herod's persecution. Matthew 2:13–18

The family returns to the hometown of Nazareth. Matthew 2:19–21

Jesus grows up in Nazareth. Matthew 2:22–23

At age 12, Jesus amazes teachers of the Jewish law. Luke 2:41–50

AD 27

Jesus is baptized by John the Baptist. Matthew 3:13–17

Jesus is tempted by Satan but does not sin. Matthew 4:1–11

Jesus calls his first disciples. John 1:38–51

Jesus changes water to wine (first miracle). John 2:6–10

Jesus is in Jerusalem for the annual Passover celebration. John 2:13

Jesus cleanses the temple of sellers who had made the holy place into a market. John 2:14–16

At Cana, Jesus heals a royal official's son. John 4:46–53

Jesus ministers in Galilee. Matthew 4:13–17

AD 28

Jesus reads from Isaiah and is rejected. Luke 4:14–30

Jesus heals people with various diseases and those possessed by demons. Luke 4:31–41

Jesus heals and forgives the sins of a paralyzed man. Luke 5:17–26

Jesus is in Jerusalem for Passover. John 5:1

Jesus heals a crippled man at the Pool of Bethesda in Jerusalem. John 5:2–9

Jesus calls the tax-collector, Levi (Matthew), to be his follower. Luke 5:27–32

The Sermon on the Mount and the Beatitudes. Matthew 5:1–7:29

Jesus heals a centurion's servant. Matthew 8:5–13

Jesus raises a widow's son from the dead. Luke 7:12–15

Jesus calms a storm. Luke 8:22–25

Jesus heals Jairus's daughter and the woman with a hemorrhage. Mark 5:21–43

Jesus heals a blind man. Matthew 9:27–34

AD 29

Jesus sends out the 12 apostles to heal diseases and drive out evil spirits. Matthew 10:1–42

The teachers of the law accuse Jesus of being out of his mind and using Satan's power. Mark 3:20–27

King Herod beheads John the Baptist. Matthew 14:3–12

The 12 apostles return. Luke 9:10

Jesus miraculously feeds 5,000 people with five loaves of bread and two fish. Mark 6:38–44

Jesus walks on water. Matthew 14:25

Jesus is in Jerusalem for Passover. John 6:4

AD 29

Jesus heals a deaf man who cannot speak. Mark 7:32–37
Jesus restores sight to a blind man. Mark 8:22–26
Peter declares that Jesus is the Son of God. Matthew 16:13–20
Jesus predicts his death. Matthew 16:21–28
The Transfiguration. Luke 9:29–36
Jesus heals a boy with an evil spirit. Mark 9:17–27
Jesus again predicts his death. Matthew 17:22–23
Jesus sends out 72 disciples. Luke 10:1–16
Jesus forgives a woman caught in adultery. John 7:53–8:11
Jesus heals a man born blind. John 9:1–41

AD 30

Jesus heals a crippled woman. Luke 13:11–13
Jesus raises Lazarus from the dead. John 11:1–46
Jesus heals 10 men with leprosy, but only one returns to give thanks. John 11:1–46
Jesus predicts his death for a third time. Matthew 20:17–19
Jesus heals blind Bartimaeus. Mark 10:46–52
Jesus stays with Zacchaeus, a wealthy and repentant man. Luke 19:1–10
Mary anoints the feet of Jesus. John 12:1–9

Palm Sunday and the week following
Palm Sunday: Jesus triumphantly enters Jerusalem.
Monday: Jesus clears the temple.
Tuesday: Jesus teaches in parables.
Wednesday: Jesus rests.
Thursday: Jesus celebrates Passover, the Last Supper, and is betrayed by his disciple Judas Iscariot.
Friday: Jesus is arrested by Roman authorities, crucified on the cross, and buried in a tomb.
Friday afternoon, Saturday, Sunday morning: Jesus' body lies in the tomb.
Sunday: Jesus rises from the dead.

Appearance of the Risen Christ
Jesus' tomb found empty by the women. Luke 24:1–8
Jesus appears to Mary Magdalene. John 20:11–18
Jesus appears on the road to Emmaus. Luke 24:13–35
Jesus appears to 10 of his disciples. John 20:19–24
Thomas doubts, but is convinced when he sees and touches the risen Christ. John 20:26–28
Jesus appears to 500 people at the same time. 1 Corinthians 15:6
Jesus instructs Peter as Jesus prepares to leave his disciples. John 21:15–53
Jesus gives the Great Commission and ascends to heaven. Luke 24:50–53

This dating assumes Jesus was born approximately 4 BC. All dates are approximate.

What Jesus said about:

LOVE

"Love the Lord your God with all your heart and with all your soul and with all your mind and with all your strength. Love your neighbor as yourself. There is no commandment greater than these."
—Mark 12:30–31

"Do to others as you would have them do to you.... Love your enemies, do good to them, and lend to them without expecting to get anything back. Then your reward will be great, and you will be sons of the Most High, because he is kind to the ungrateful and wicked. Be merciful, just as your Father is merciful."—Luke 6:31–36

"A new command I give you: Love one another. As I have loved you, so you must love one another. By this all men will know that you are my disciples, if you love one another."—John 13:34–35

"Whoever has my commands and obeys them, he is the one who loves me. He who loves me will be loved by my Father, and I too will love him and show myself to him."—John 14:21

GOD

"Do not let your hearts be troubled. Trust in God; trust also in me."
—John 14:1

"[The disciples] were greatly astonished and asked, 'Who then can be saved?' Jesus looked at them and said, 'With man this is impossible, but with God all things are possible.'"—Matthew 19:25–26

"If God were your Father, you would love me, for I came from God and now am here. I have not come on my own; but he sent me."—John 8:42

ETERNAL LIFE

"Now this is eternal life: that they may know you, the only true God, and Jesus Christ whom you have sent."—John 17:3

"I tell you the truth, whoever hears my word and believes him who sent me has eternal life and will not be condemned; he has crossed over from death to life."—John 5:24

"If anyone would come after me, he must deny himself and take up his cross and follow me. For whoever wants to save his life will lose it, but whoever loses his life for me and for the gospel will save it."—Mark 8:34–36

Denominations
Comparison

12 Major Denominations
Beliefs and Practices

Catholic Church

When was it founded and by whom?	Catholics consider Jesus' disciple Peter (died c. AD 66) the first pope; Gregory the Great (pope, AD 540–604) was a key figure in the pope's office. At that time, the pope came to be viewed as ruling over the whole church.
How many adherents?*	About 1 billion worldwide; 62 million, USA
How is Scripture viewed?	The Scriptures teach without error the truth needed for our salvation. Scripture must be interpreted within the Tradition of the Church. The canon includes 46 books for the Old Testament including deuterocanonical books (the Apocrypha) and 27 books for the New Testament.
Who is God?	The one Creator and Lord of all, existing eternally as the Trinity (Father, Son, and Holy Spirit).
Who is Jesus?	The eternal Son incarnate, fully God and fully man, conceived and born of the Virgin Mary, died on the cross for our sins, rose bodily from the grave, ascended into heaven, and will come again in glory to judge us all.
How are we saved?	Christ died as a substitutionary sacrifice for our sins; God by his grace infuses a supernatural gift of faith in Christ in those who are baptized, which is maintained by doing works of love and receiving Penance and the Eucharist.
What happens after death?	The souls of the faithful go to heaven either immediately or, if imperfectly purified in this life, after purgatory. The souls of the wicked at death are immediately consigned to eternal punishment in hell.
What is the church?	The church is the Mystical Body of Christ, established by Christ with the bishop of Rome (the pope), who may at times pronounce dogma (doctrine required of all members) infallibly, as its earthly head. It is united (*one*) in a sacred (*holy*) worldwide (*catholic*) community through the succession of bishops whose ordination goes back to the apostles (*apostolic*); Christians not in communion with the Catholic Church are called "separated brethren."
What about the sacraments?	Baptism removes original sin (usually in infants). In the Eucharist, the substances (but not the properties) of bread and wine are changed into Jesus' body and blood (transubstantiation).
What are other beliefs and practices of note?	Mary was conceived by her mother immaculately (free of original sin), remained a virgin perpetually, and was assumed bodily into heaven. She is the Mother of the Church and is considered an object of devotion and veneration (a show of honor that stops short of worship).
What are the major divisions or trends today?	About one-fourth of Catholics are doctrinally conservative. Many priests and members tend to accept liberal, pluralist beliefs contrary to church teaching.

*Figures as of year 2000

Orthodox Churches

Date	AD 330: Emperor Constantine renamed the city of Byzantium "Constantinople," which became the city of the leading patriarch in the "Great Schism" of 1054.
No.	About 225 million worldwide; 3–5 million, USA
Scripture	The Scriptures are without error in matters of faith only. Scripture is to be interpreted by Sacred Tradition, especially the seven Ecumenical Councils which met from AD 325–787. The canon includes 49 Old Testament books (the Catholic Bible plus three more) and the 27 New Testament books.
God	The one Creator and Lord of all, existing eternally as the Trinity (Father, Son, and Holy Spirit).
Jesus	The eternal Son incarnate, fully God and fully man, conceived and born of the Virgin Mary, died on the cross for our sins, rose bodily from the grave, ascended into heaven, and will come again in glory to judge us all.
Salvation	In Christ, God became human so that human beings might be deified (*theosis*), that is, have the energy of God's life in them. Through baptism and participation in the church, God's people receive the benefits of Christ's redeeming work as they persevere.
Death	At death, the souls of the faithful are purified as needed (a process of growth, not punishment), then get a foretaste of eternal blessing in heaven. The souls of the wicked get a foretaste of eternal torment in hell.
The Church	The church is the Body of Christ in unbroken historical connection to the apostles, changelessly maintaining the faith of the undivided church as expressed in the creeds. It is one, holy, catholic, and apostolic, with churches organized nationally (Armenian, Greek, Russian, and so forth) with its bishops under the leadership of patriarchs (the pope being recognized as one of several), of which that of Constantinople has primacy of honor.
Sacraments	Baptism initiates God's life in the one baptized (usually infants). In the Eucharist, bread and wine are changed into Jesus' body and blood (a Mystery to be left unexplained).
Beliefs	Mary conceived Jesus virginally. She remained a virgin perpetually, and (in tradition, not dogma) was assumed bodily into heaven. Icons (images of Christ, Mary, or the saints) are objects of veneration through which God is to be worshiped.
Trends	A significant proportion are doctrinally conservative. Most Orthodox bodies are members of the World Council of Churches, whose liberal leanings have long caused concern.

Lutheran Churches

Date	1517: Martin Luther's "95 Theses" (challenges to Catholic teaching) usually mark the beginning of the Protestant Reformation. 1530: The Augsburg Confession is the first formal Lutheran statement of faith.
No.	About 60 million worldwide (all branches; see below); over 8 million, USA
Scripture	Scripture alone is the authoritative witness to the gospel (some parts more directly or fully than others). Conservatives view Scripture as inerrant. The standard Protestant canon of 39 Old Testament books and 27 New Testament books is accepted.
God	The one Creator and Lord of all, existing eternally as the Trinity (Father, Son, and Holy Spirit).
Jesus	The eternal Son incarnate, fully God and fully man, conceived and born of the Virgin Mary, died on the cross for our sins, rose bodily from the grave, ascended into heaven, and will come again in glory to judge us all.
Salvation	We are saved by grace alone when God imputes to us his gift of righteousness through faith alone (*sola fide*) in Christ, who died for our sins. Good works are the inevitable result of true faith, but in no way the basis of our right standing before God.
Death	The souls of believers upon dying go immediately to be with Christ, and at Christ's return, their bodies are raised to immortal, eternal life. The souls of the wicked begin suffering immediately in hell. 
The Church	The church is the congregation of believers (though mixed with the lost) in which the gospel is taught and the sacraments rightly administered. All believers are "priests" in that they have direct access to God. All ministers are pastors; some serve as bishops. Historically, apostolic succession has been rejected.
Sacraments	Baptism is necessary for salvation; in it both adults and infants are given God's grace. The Lord's Supper remains truly bread and wine but also becomes truly Jesus' body and blood (consubstantiation).
Beliefs	The church's liturgy is similar to the Episcopal. Conservative Lutherans generally affirm that God chooses who will be saved before they believe. In 2009 the ELCA opened the ministry to gay and lesbian pastors in committed relationships.
Trends	The Evangelical Lutheran Church in America (ELCA) is the mainline church. In 1999 the ELCA approved full communion with the Episcopal Church. The Lutheran Church—Missouri Synod is doctrinally conservative.

Anglican Churches (Episcopal)

Date	1534: King Henry VIII was declared head of the Church of England. 1549: Thomas Cranmer produced the first Book of Common Prayer.
No.	Some 45–75 million worldwide; 2.3 million, USA
Scripture	Scripture contains the truth that is necessary for salvation and is the primary norm for faith, but must be interpreted in light of tradition and reason. The canon includes 39 Old Testament books and 27 New Testament books (the Apocrypha is respected but not viewed as Scripture).
God	The one Creator and Lord of all, existing eternally as the Trinity (Father, Son, and Holy Spirit).
Jesus	The eternal Son incarnate, fully God and fully man, conceived and born of the Virgin Mary, died on the cross for our sins, rose bodily from the grave, ascended into heaven, and will come again in glory to judge us all.
Salvation	Christ suffered and died as an offering for sin, freeing us from sin and reconciling us to God; we share in Christ's victory when in baptism we become living members of the church, believing in him and keeping his commandments.
Death	The souls of the faithful are purified as needed to enjoy full communion with God, and at Christ's return they are raised to the fullness of eternal life in heaven. Those who reject God face eternal death.
The Church	The church is the Body of Christ, whose unity is based on the "apostolic succession" of bishops going back to the apostles, of whom the bishop of Rome is one of many. It is one, holy, catholic, and apostolic. The Anglican communion is a part of the church, whose unity worldwide is represented by the archbishop of Canterbury. The church in the USA is known as the Episcopal Church.
Sacraments	The sacraments are "outward and visible signs of an inward and spiritual grace." Infants and converts are made part of the church in baptism. Christ's body and blood are really present in Communion. Canterbury Cathedral, England
Beliefs	Members are free to accept or reject the Catholic doctrines of Mary. The Book of Common Prayer is the norm for liturgy. Priests may marry. In 1976 the Episcopal Church approved the ordination of women. In 2009 the Episcopal Church approved the ordination of gay bishops and allowed bishops to bless same-sex unions.
Trends	In the USA, most belong to the Episcopal Church. About one-fifth are doctrinally conservative. The 39 Articles (1571) are the doctrinal basis for conservative splinter groups, such as the Reformed Episcopal Church and the Anglican Church in North America.

Presbyterian Churches

Date	1536: John Calvin writes *Institutes of the Christian Religion.* 1643–49: Westminster Standards define Presbyterian doctrine. 1789: Presbyterian Church (USA) first organized (see below).
No.	Some 40–48 million worldwide; 3–4 million, USA
Scripture	Historic view: Scripture is inspired and infallible, the sole, final rule of faith. PCUSA: Scripture is "the witness without parallel" to Christ, but in merely human words reflecting beliefs of the time. The standard Protestant canon is accepted.
God	The one Creator and Lord of all, existing eternally as the Trinity (Father, Son, and Holy Spirit).
Jesus	The eternal Son incarnate, fully God and fully man, conceived and born of the Virgin Mary, died on the cross for our sins, rose bodily from the grave, ascended into heaven, and will come again in glory to judge us all.
Salvation	We are saved by grace alone when God imputes to us his gift of righteousness through faith alone (*sola fide*) in Christ, who died for our sins. Good works are the inevitable result of true faith, but in no way the basis of our right standing before God.
Death	The souls of believers upon dying go immediately to be with Christ. At Christ's return, their bodies are raised to immortal, eternal life. The souls of the wicked begin suffering immediately in hell.
The Church	The church is the body of Christ, including all whom God has chosen as his people, represented by the visible church, composed of churches that vary in purity and corruption. Christ alone is the head of the church. Congregations choose elders to govern them. Regional groups of elders (presbyteries) meet in denomination-wide General Assemblies.
Sacraments	Baptism is not necessary for salvation but is a sign of the new covenant of grace, for adults and infants. Jesus' body and blood are spiritually present to believers in the Lord's Supper.
Beliefs	Conservatives affirm the "five points of Calvinism": humans are so sinful that they cannot initiate return to God; God chooses who will be saved; Christ died specifically to save those whom God chose; God infallibly draws to Christ those whom he chooses; they will never fall away.
Trends	The Presbyterian Church (USA), or PCUSA, is the mainline church. The Presbyterian Church in America (PCA) is the largest doctrinally conservative church body.

John Calvin

Methodist Churches

Date	1738: Conversion of John and Charles Wesley, already devout Anglican ministers, sparks Great Awakening. 1784: USA Methodists form separate church body.
No.	Some 20–40 million worldwide; 12 million or more, USA
Scripture	Historic view: Scripture is inspired and infallible, the sole, final rule of faith. United Methodist Church: Scripture is "the primary source and criterion for Christian doctrine," but (for most) not infallible. The standard Protestant canon is accepted.
God	The one Creator and Lord of all, existing eternally as the Trinity (Father, Son, and Holy Spirit).
Jesus	The eternal Son incarnate, fully God and fully man, conceived and born of the virgin Mary, died on the cross for our sins, rose bodily from the grave, ascended into heaven, and will come again in glory to judge us all.
Salvation	We are saved by grace alone when God regenerates and forgives us through faith in Christ, who died for our sins. Good works are the necessary result of true faith, but do not obtain forgiveness or salvation.
Death	The souls of believers upon dying go immediately to be with Christ; and, at Christ's return, their bodies are raised to immortal, eternal life. The wicked will suffer eternal punishment in hell.
The Church	The church is the body of Christ, represented by visible church institutions. Bishops oversee regions and appoint pastors. In the United Methodist Church, clergy and laity meet together in a national "General Conference" every four years. All pastors are itinerant, meaning they move from one church to the next as directed by the bishop (on average once every four years).
Sacraments	Baptism is a sign of regeneration and of the new covenant and is for adults and children. Jesus is really present, and his body and blood are spiritually present, to believers in the Lord's Supper.
Beliefs	"Entire sanctification" is a work of the Spirit subsequent to regeneration by which fully consecrated believers are purified of all sin and fit for service—a state maintained by faith and obedience. Methodists are Arminian, i.e., they disagree with all five points of Calvinism.
Trends	United Methodist Church (8.5 million) and the African Methodist Episcopal church bodies (about 4 million) are mainline churches. The Free Methodists are a small conservative body.

John Wesley

Anabaptist Churches

Date	1525: Protestants in Zurich begin believer's baptism. 1537: Menno Simons begins leading Mennonite movement. 1682: A Quaker, William Penn, founds Pennsylvania.
No.	Perhaps 2 million worldwide; Roughly 600,000, USA.
Scripture	Most view Scripture as the inspired means for knowing and following Jesus, but not as infallible. Jesus is the living Word. Scripture is the written Word that points to him. The standard Protestant canon is accepted. How believers live is emphasized over having correct doctrine.
God	The one Creator and Lord of all, revealed in Jesus through the Holy Spirit. Most affirm the Trinity in some way.
Jesus	The Savior of the world, a man in whom God's love and will are revealed by his life of service and his suffering and death. His deity, virgin birth, and resurrection are traditionally affirmed.
Salvation	Salvation is a personal experience in which, through faith in Jesus, we become at peace with God, moving us to follow Jesus' example as his disciples by living as peacemakers in the world.
Death	No official view of what happens immediately after death. At Christ's return God's people will be raised to eternal life and the unrepentant will be forever separated from God (the traditional view).
The Church	The church is the body of Christ, the assembly and society of Christ's disciples who follow him in the power of the Spirit. It is to be marked by holiness, love, service, a simple lifestyle, and peacemaking. No one system of church government is recognized; leadership is to be characterized by humble service and is primarily but not exclusively local.
Sacraments	Baptism is for believers only, a sign of commitment to follow Jesus. The Lord's Supper is a memorial of his death. Most Quakers view sacraments as spiritual only, not external rites.
Beliefs	Anabaptists and similar bodies are "peace churches," teaching nonresistance and pacifism (the view that all participation in war is wrong). Doctrine is de-emphasized, and liberal views with social emphasis prevail in some church bodies, including most Quaker churches.
Trends	The Mennonite Church and Church of the Brethren are the largest bodies; the Amish (1693) are a variety of Mennonites. Quakers (Friends) originated separately but share much in common with Anabaptists.

Congregational Churches

Date	1607: Members of a house church in England, illegal at that time, who were forced into exile. 1620: Congregationalists called Pilgrims sail on *Mayflower* to Plymouth (now in Massachusetts).
No.	Over 2 million worldwide; About 2 million, USA.
Scripture	Most view Scripture as "the authoritative witness to the Word of God" that was living in Jesus, rather than viewing Scripture as the unerring Word of God. (UCC, see below.) The Bible and creeds are seen as "testimonies of faith, not tests of faith." The standard Protestant canon is accepted.
God	The Eternal Spirit who calls the worlds into being and is made known in the man Jesus.
Jesus	The crucified and risen Savior and Lord, in whom we are reconciled to God. (His deity and virgin birth are widely ignored or rejected except in the conservative church bodies.)
Salvation	God promises forgiveness and grace to save "from sin and aimlessness" all who trust him, who accept his call to serve the whole human family.
Death	Those who trust in God and live as Jesus' disciples are promised eternal life in God's kingdom. No position is taken on the future of the wicked (most reject the idea of eternal punishment).
The Church	The church is the people of God living as Jesus' disciples by serving humanity as agents of God's reconciling love. Each local church is self-governing and chooses its own ministers. The United Church of Christ is not part of the "Churches of Christ" but was formed in 1957 as the union of the Congregational Christian Churches and the Evangelical and Reformed Church, a liberal Protestant body.
Sacraments	Congregations may practice infant baptism or believer's baptism or both. Sacraments are symbols of spiritual realities.
Beliefs	The United Church of Christ (UCC) is one of the most theologically liberal denominations in the USA. Individual ministers and churches vary widely in belief. The United Church of Christ ordains openly homosexual men and women to ministry.
Trends	United Church of Christ (1.5 million) is staunchly liberal. The National Association of Congregational Christian Churches (110,000) is a mainline body. The Conservative Congregational Christian Conference (38,000) is evangelical.

Baptist Churches

Date	1612: John Smythe and other English Puritans form the first Baptist church. 1639: The first Baptist church in America established in Providence, Rhode Island.
No.	100 million worldwide (including families); 25–30 million, USA.
Scripture	Scripture is inspired and without error, the sole, final, totally trustworthy rule of faith. The standard Protestant canon is accepted. (Mainline churches vary in the extent to which they continue to view Scripture as without error.) 
God	The one Creator and Lord of all, existing eternally as the Trinity (Father, Son, and Holy Spirit).
Jesus	The eternal Son incarnate, fully God and fully human, conceived and born of the Virgin Mary, died on the cross for our sins, rose bodily from the grave, ascended into heaven, and will come again in glory to judge us all.
Salvation	We are saved by grace alone when God imputes to us his gift of righteousness through faith alone (*sola fide*) in Christ, who died for our sins. Good works are the inevitable result of true faith, but in no way the basis of our right standing before God.
Death	The souls of believers upon dying go immediately to be with Christ; and, at Christ's return, their bodies are raised to immortal, eternal life. The wicked will suffer eternal punishment in hell.
The Church	The church (universal) is the body of Christ, which consists of the redeemed throughout history. The term "church" usually refers to local congregations, each of which is autonomous, whose members are to be baptized believers and whose officers are pastors and deacons. Churches may form associations or conventions for cooperative purposes, especially missions and education.
Sacraments	Baptism is immersion of believers only as a symbol of their faith in Christ. The Lord's Supper is a symbolic memorial of Christ's death and anticipation of his return. 
Beliefs	Most Baptist bodies emphasize evangelism and missions. Church and state are to be separate. Baptists include both Calvinists (dominant in the Southern Baptist Convention) and Arminians (dominant in mainline bodies and the Free-Will Baptist bodies).
Trends	Southern Baptist (15 million), a conservative body, are the largest Protestant denomination in the USA. American Baptists (1.5 million) and the National Baptists (5–8 million) are mainline churches.

Churches of Christ

Date	1801: Barton Stone holds his Cane Ridge Revival in Kentucky. 1832: Stone's Christians unite with Thomas and Alexander Campbell's Disciples of Christ. They have different beliefs in some areas.
No.	Perhaps 5–6 million worldwide; 3–4 million, USA.
Scripture	"Where the Scriptures speak, we speak; where the Scriptures are silent, we are silent." Churches of Christ view Scripture as the inerrant word of God; Disciples of Christ generally view Scripture as witness to Christ but fallible. The standard Protestant canon is accepted.
God	The one Creator and Lord of all. The creeds are rejected, but most conservatives accept the idea of the Trinity.
Jesus	The Son of God, fully God and fully human, conceived and born of the Virgin Mary, died on the cross for our sins, rose bodily from the grave, ascended into heaven, and will come again in glory to judge us all.
Salvation	Churches of Christ: A person must hear the gospel, believe in Christ, repent, confess Christ, be baptized, and persevere in holiness to be saved. Disciples of Christ: God saves human beings (possibly all) by his grace, to which we respond in faith.
Death	Churches of Christ: Believers immediately go to be with Christ and at his return are raised to immortality; the wicked will suffer eternally in hell. Disciples: Most believe in personal immortality but not hell.
The Church	Churches of Christ: The church is the assembly of those who have responded rightly to the gospel; it must be called only by the name of Christ. Only such churches are part of the restoration of true Christianity. Each local church is autonomous and calls its own pastors. Disciples of Christ have a similar form of church government but are ecumenical, and thus do not claim to be the sole restoration of true Christianity.
Sacraments	Baptism is immersion of believers only, as the initial act of obedience to the gospel. Many Churches of Christ recognize baptism in their own churches only as valid. The Lord's Supper is a symbolic memorial.
Beliefs	Many but not all Churches of Christ forbid the use of instrumental music in worship. International Churches of Christ teaches that its members alone are saved and is widely reported to strongly influence its members.
Trends	Churches of Christ (about 2 million) are conservative, some militantly and others not. Christian Church (Disciples of Christ) (about 1 million) is the mainline church body.

Adventist Churches

Date	1844: William Miller's prediction that Christ's "advent" (return) would occur in 1844 failed. It was later interpreted as a heavenly event, not as an actual return. 1863: Seventh-day Adventist Church is organized.
No.	Over 18 million worldwide (plus members of much smaller bodies); over 1 million, USA.
Scripture	Scripture is inspired and without error, the final, totally trustworthy rule of faith. The standard Protestant canon is accepted. *The Clear Word* paraphrase is favored. Ellen G. White, an early Seventh-day Adventist leader, was a prophet; her writings are a "continuing and authoritative source of truth."

Ellen G. White

God	The one Creator and Lord of all, "a unity of three co-eternal Persons" (Father, Son, and Holy Spirit).
Jesus	The eternal Son incarnate, fully God and fully human, conceived and born of the Virgin Mary, died on the cross for our sins, rose bodily from the grave, ascended into heaven, and will come again in glory to judge us all.
Salvation	To be saved, we repent, believe in Christ as Example (in his life) and Substitute (by his death), and so by grace are made right with God and sanctified and empowered by the Spirit to live in obedience to God's commandments. Those found obedient at the end will be saved.
Death	Death for all people is an unconscious state. At Christ's return the righteous will be raised for life in heaven. After a Millennium, the wicked will be raised only to be annihilated; the righteous will live forever on a new earth.
The Church	The universal church includes all who believe in Christ. The last days are a time of apostasy during which a remnant (the Seventh-day Adventist Church) keeps God's commandments faithfully. The General Conference, composed of delegates from regional "union missions," governs the whole church.
Sacraments	Baptism is by immersion and is contingent upon affirmation both of faith in Jesus and Adventist doctrines. Baptism is into the Seventh-day Adventist Church. The Lord's Supper is a symbolic memorial of Christ's death, is practiced quarterly, and follows foot-washing.
Beliefs	In 1844 Christ began the "Investigative Judgment," a work in heaven of determining who among the dead and living are true, loyal believers obeying God's law. Rest and worship on Saturday is an essential element of that obedience. When the Judgment work is done, Christ will return.
Trends	The Seventh-day Adventist Church is by far the largest body, followed by SDA Reform Movement. Most of the smaller offshoots reject the Trinity and other historic Christian doctrines.

Pentecostal Churches

Date	1901: Charles Fox Parham's Kansas Bethel Bible College students speak in tongues. 1906: The Azusa Street revival (led by William J. Seymor in Los Angeles) launches Pentecostal movement. 1914: Assemblies of God organize.
No.	500 million worldwide (estimates vary); roughly 10 million, USA.
Scripture	Scripture is inspired and without error, the final, totally trustworthy rule of faith. The standard Protestant canon is accepted. Some church bodies view certain leaders as prophets with authoritative messages that are to be confirmed from Scripture.
God	The one Creator and Lord of all, existing eternally as the Trinity (Father, Son, and Holy Spirit).
Jesus	The eternal Son incarnate, fully God and fully human, conceived and born of the Virgin Mary, died on the cross for our sins, rose bodily from the grave, ascended into heaven, and will come again in glory to judge us all.
Salvation	We are saved by God's grace, by Christ's death for our sins, through repentance and faith in Christ alone, resulting in our being born again to new life in the Spirit, as evidenced by a life of holiness.
Death	The souls of believers upon dying go immediately to be with Christ, and at Christ's return their bodies are raised to immortal, eternal life. The wicked will suffer eternal punishment in hell.
The Church	The church is the body of Christ, in which the Holy Spirit dwells, which meets to worship God, and which is the agency for bringing the gospel of salvation to the whole world. Most church bodies practice a form of church government similar to Baptists.
Sacraments	Baptism is immersion of believers only, as a symbol of their faith in Christ. The Lord's Supper is a symbolic memorial of Christ's death and anticipation of his return.
Beliefs	Pentecostals in the strict sense view speaking in tongues as the initial evidence of baptism in the Holy Spirit (a second work of grace akin to entire sanctification in Methodism). Charismatics accept tongues but don't view it as the only initial evidence of baptism in the Holy Spirit.
Trends	Assemblies of God (2.5 million USA, historically white) and Church of God in Christ (3 million USA, historically black) are the largest church bodies. "Oneness" churches reject the Trinity.

Terms & Definitions

ANABAPTIST Literally, "one who is baptized again." (1) Groups that baptize believers who were already baptized as infants. Anabaptists deny that they are doing so, since in their view infant baptism is not valid. (2) Specifically, the Anabaptists of Zurich and the church bodies (e.g., Mennonites, Amish) that trace their heritage to them.

APOCRYPHA Books considered part of the Old Testament in Catholic or Orthodox theology but not in Protestant theology (e.g., 1 and 2 Maccabees, Wisdom of Solomon). Called *deuterocanonical* in Catholic theology.

APOSTOLIC SUCCESSION The doctrine that there is an unbroken line of succession from the original apostles of Jesus Christ to bishops of today. Only bishops in proper succession may ordain priests authorized to perform the sacraments.

ARMINIAN (1) In the theological tradition of Jacob Arminius (1560–1609), a theologian in early Dutch Calvinism who broke with the Calvinist mainstream on matters pertaining to predestination. (2) Somewhat loosely, any Protestant who rejects the Calvinist view of predestination and related doctrines (especially most Anglicans, Methodists, Churches of Christ, and Pentecostals).

CALVINIST (1) In the theological tradition of John Calvin (1509–64), particularly in the Reformed and Presbyterian church bodies. (2) Somewhat loosely, any Protestant who holds to the Calvinist view of predestination and related doctrines, including some Baptists and other evangelicals. Conservative Lutherans are closer to Calvinism than to Arminianism, but differ in relatively minor ways. 3) Five points of Calvinism: humans are so sinful that they cannot initiate return to God; God chooses who will be saved; Christ died specifically to save those whom God chose; God infallibly draws to Christ those whom he chooses; they will never fall away.

CANON Authoritative list of books belonging in the Bible (or in the Old or New Testament).

CATHOLIC Literally, "universal" (1) The faithful church in all its expressions worldwide. (2) *Capitalized*. Having to do with the church body headed by the Pope.

CHARISMATIC (1) A generic term for spiritual enablement, as in, *charismatic gifts* (tongues, healings, prophecies, etc.). (2) Church bodies whose members practice speaking in tongues and other charismatic gifts but that do not view tongues as the initial evidence of having received the baptism in the Holy Spirit. (3) Christians in other denominations who experience charismatic gifts.

CLERGY Priests, ministers, pastors, and other official church leaders, usually said to be *ordained* (specially recognized as having a spiritual responsibility as a leader in the church). *Antonym*: laity.

CONFESSION (1) A document stating what a particular church body or other group of Christians believe in common, such as the Augsburg Confession (Lutheran) or the Westminster Confession of Faith (Presbyterian). (2) The act of privately telling a priest about one's sins (see *Penance*).

CONGREGATIONAL (1) A form of church government in which each local church is self-governing; practiced by many denominational groups. (2) *Capitalized*. A church tradition originating in Puritan England that was congregational in church government but (unlike most others) also accepted infant baptism.

CONSERVATIVE Retaining the theological position enshrined in the church body's historic creeds or confessions. *Antonym*: liberal.

CONVERSION (1) The act of changing from one religion (or none) to a new religion, as in conversion from Buddhism to Christianity. (2) The experience of coming to personal faith in Christ, even if the person was already a member of a Christian church.

ECUMENICAL Literally, "of the world." (1) Representing the Christian church before the schism between the Eastern and Western churches; especially, the creeds and councils of the first millennium. (2) Seeking to foster institutional cooperation or even unity among all Christian church bodies (or at least among some).

EUCHARIST Literally, "thanksgiving." Term of choice in liturgical churches for Communion or the Lord's Supper.

EVANGELICAL (1) Conservative Christians, mostly Protestant, who affirm the infallibility or inerrancy of the Bible. (2) *Capitalized*. Church bodies in the tradition of Martin Luther (1483–1546), whether or not they are evangelical in the generic sense.

HELL (1) *Capitalized*. In Christian theology, the final state of the wicked, that is, of the devil, all fallen angels, and all human beings not redeemed by Christ. (2) In the King James Version of the Bible, "hell" translates both the Greek *Gehenna* (which does refer to the final state of the wicked) and the Greek *Hades* (which refers to the temporary waiting place of all departed human beings between their death and resurrection).

HOLINESS (1) God's attribute of sinless perfection, of being beyond and above all impurity or evil an attribute that human beings are meant to have but do not because of sin. (2) *Capitalized*. The Christian tradition, stemming from John Wesley, which believes that Christians need a distinct work or effect of God's grace in their lives that makes them personally holy and ready for Christian love and service; or, any of the several denominations in that tradition (e.g., Christian & Missionary Alliance, Nazarenes, Salvation Army).

IMMERSION A form of baptism in which a person is completely submerged under water; nearly always practiced in Baptist churches.

IMMORTALITY A state in which a person is unable to die, certain to live forever.

INCARNATE, INCARNATION Literally, "in the flesh." The doctrine that Jesus, who was God the Son, "became flesh" (John 1:14), that is, became a fully human being, while still being also fully God.

INERRANT Without error; used by evangelicals with reference to the complete trustworthiness of the Bible in all matters on which it speaks.

INFALLIBLE Without error, sometimes understood comprehensively (as in *inerrant*) and sometimes viewed as limited to certain areas or subjects (especially faith and morals). Applied in Catholic theology to the pope in certain specific pronouncements, and applied in conservative Catholic and Protestant theology alike to the Bible.

LAITY All church members not holding official church leadership offices. *Antonym*: clergy.

LIBERAL Theological views that deny the infallibility of the Bible and that question, in varying degrees, the traditional doctrines held in common by most Christians prior to the modern era (such as the Virgin Birth or the Trinity). *Antonym*: conservative.

LITURGICAL, LITURGY A form of corporate worship in which the priest or minister leads the congregation in readings and prayers from a prescribed text (called the *liturgy*).

MAINLINE A Protestant denomination generally originating before 1900 (though it may have undergone recent mergers), from which theologically conservative congregations have separated (e.g., the United Methodist Church).

NEW COVENANT The relationship binding believers in Christ to him that in some way superseded the "old covenant" that God had made with Israel through Moses (see 2 Corinthians 3), into which a person enters in baptism and which is celebrated in the Lord's Supper.

ORDINANCE Term of choice primarily in non-liturgical churches for baptism and the Lord's Supper; is understood to mean that the rite is a symbol of God's grace already present in the believer. See *sacrament.*

ORTHODOX (1) Adhering to the essentials of the Christian faith, especially as articulated in the early creeds; in this sense the "orthodox" include conservative Catholics, Protestants, and Orthodox. (2) *Capitalized.* Having to do with the association of church bodies of Eastern Europe and the Middle East that became divided from Rome and the churches aligned with it in Western Europe in the "Great Schism" of 1054.

PATRIARCH In the Orthodox Churches, the bishop recognized as the leader of all Orthodox bishops under his jurisdiction (usually a nation or ethnic group, such as Greeks, Armenians, or Russians).

PENANCE The Catholic sacrament in which a person confesses his sins to a priest and is given assurance of forgiveness.

POPE The title, meaning "Father," referring to the Bishop of Rome (head of the Roman Catholic Church).

PREDESTINATION A term used by Paul of God's prior decision that determines who is saved. Calvinists hold that God predestines individuals and on that basis brings them to faith; Arminians and most other Christian bodies hold that God predetermines that those who believe will be saved, but does not predetermine who will believe.

PROTESTANT REFORMATION The movement originally calling for reform of the doctrines, preaching, and rites of the Catholic Church, ignited by the work of Martin Luther, and which resulted in the secession of many churches from the Catholic Church. All of the church bodies profiled in the chart are Protestant except for the Catholic and Orthodox churches (although the Anglican Church also regards itself as Catholic).

PURGATORY A state or place to which believers go after death to have any remaining sin or impurity purged or removed before going to heaven. In the Catholic Church this is generally regarded as a place of temporal punishment; it is not so regarded in the Orthodox and Anglican churches. Most Protestants do not believe in Purgatory but rather in an immediate purgation of sin at death.

PURITAN English Protestants who embraced Reformed (Calvinist) theology and wanted to purify the Church of England from supposed corruption, especially ornate church decor and priestly garments.

SACRAMENT Term of choice primarily in liturgical churches for baptism and the Lord's Supper (and, for Catholics, five other rites); is understood to mean that the rite is in some way a means by which God extends his grace. See *ordinance.*

SANCTIFICATION (1) Being set apart, or consecrated, to God. (2) The work of the Holy Spirit by which a believer is made holy in character.

VIRGIN BIRTH The miracle by which Mary conceived and gave birth to Jesus by the power of the Holy Spirit, without being impregnated by a man.

Author: Robert M. Bowman Jr., M.A., Director of Research at the Institute for Religious Research
Research Consultant: Eric Pement

Family Tree of Denominations

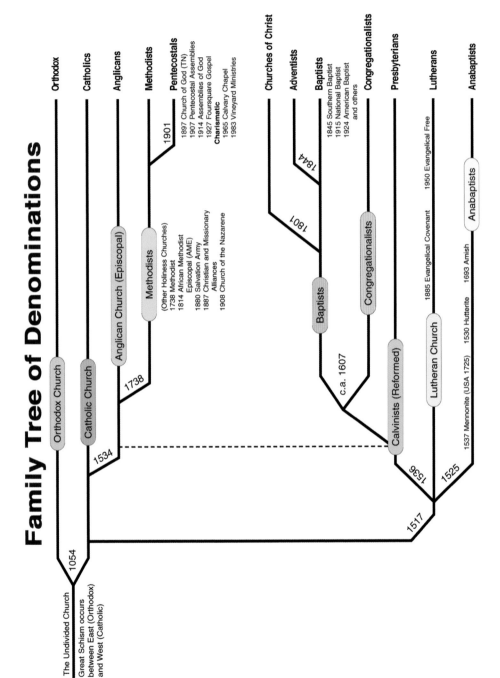

The Undivided Church

1054 — Great Schism occurs between East (Orthodox) and West (Catholic)

1517

Orthodox
Orthodox Church

Catholics
Catholic Church
1534

Anglicans
Anglican Church (Episcopal)
1534

Methodists
Methodists
1738
1901
(Other Holiness Churches)
1738 Methodist
1814 African Methodist Episcopal (AME)
1880 Salvation Army
1887 Christian and Missionary Alliances
1908 Church of the Nazarene

Pentecostals
1897 Church of God (TN)
1907 Pentecostal Assemblies
1914 Assemblies of God
1927 Foursquare Gospel
Charismatic
1965 Calvary Chapel
1983 Vineyard Ministries

Churches of Christ

Adventists
1844

Baptists
Baptists
1801
c.a. 1607
1845 Southern Baptist
1915 National Baptist
1924 American Baptist and others

Congregationalists
Congregationalists

Presbyterians
Calvinists (Reformed)
1536

Lutherans
Lutheran Church
1525
1885 Evangelical Covenant
1950 Evangelical Free

1537 Mennonite (USA 1725)   1530 Hutterite   1693 Amish

Anabaptists
Anabaptists

Baptism

History and Methods of Baptism
Old Testament Symbolism
Believer's vs. Infant Baptism

Why Be Baptized?

Baptism is one of the most important practices in the life of the church. The need for baptism is something that most Christians recognize. Jesus emphasized the importance of baptism when he commanded his disciples to "Go and make disciples of all nations, baptizing them in the name of the Father and of the Son and of the Holy Spirit" (Matthew 28:19). Baptism reminds us of

- Jesus' death and resurrection
- Our relationship to God and one another through the Holy Spirit (Ephesians 4:4-6).

Committed Christians interpret baptism in different ways, but most Christians agree that baptism

- is central to the Christian faith;
- is not optional but a commandment;
- is often a way for people to show in public their commitment to God;
- unifies Christians as members of the same body;
- has no ultimate significance apart from faith in Jesus Christ.

Baptize

The term *baptism* comes from a Greek word. The verb *baptizo* means "to cover in water, wash, dip, baptize."

What Happens During Baptism?

Although baptism ceremonies may look quite different from group to group, there are more similarities than differences.

1. Water is always present, whether it is in the form of a natural body of water, a baptismal font, a baptistery, a pool, or simply a bowl of water.
2. A church leader asks a few questions to give opportunity for persons involved in the baptism to profess their faith outwardly, then asks the support of those present. In the case of infant baptism, those questions are for the parents and others present to make certain that the child will have Christian examples, support, and instruction to guide the child toward an eventual profession (public expression) of faith.
3. The leader sprinkles, pours, or immerses the person being baptized and says, "I baptize you in the name of the Father and of the Son and of the Holy Spirit."

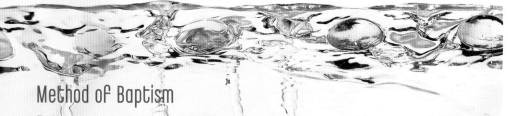

Method of Baptism

Different methods are used in baptism—some groups sprinkle water on the forehead, others pour water from a pitcher over the whole head, and others dip or immerse a person's whole body in water.

- Those who practice believers' baptism believe that the practice of immersion (being completely covered with water) more fully displays the symbolic burial of the believer's old life. As believers go under and emerge from the water, they identify themselves with Jesus' sacrificial death, burial, and resurrection (Romans 6:3–4).

- Other modes of baptism developed in the early church—such as pouring (affusion) and sprinkling (aspersion)—are more practical during times of persecution, and also with infants. As a result, pouring and sprinkling are usually connected with churches that practice infant baptism and with places where Christianity is illegal.

Believer's Baptism vs. Infant Baptism

One of the main points on which Christian groups differ is about *who* can be baptized. The following table clarifies the emphasis in perspective that each tradition places on its understanding of baptism.

Note the difference in emphasis. Both traditions agree that the act of baptism itself does not save a person. Salvation comes through Christ alone by faith (Galatians 3:26–28; Ephesians 2:8–9). Christians disagree about whether a person must be able to communicate a desire for baptism and an understanding of its meaning (sometimes referred to as the "age of accountability").

Believer's Baptism	Infant Baptism
Emphasis on faith as a human response to God's grace	Emphasis on faith as a gift from God
Believer who trusts	God who acts
Obedience and faith of believer	Command and promise of God
Believer's witness to the world	Covenant and covenant community
Old Testament model of sacrifice	Old Testament model of circumcision

Those who advocate *believer's baptism* refer to Bible passages that reveal recognition and repentance as a sign of readiness for baptism, such as:

Acts 2:38

> Peter replied, ***Repent and be baptized***, *every one of you, in the name of Jesus Christ for the forgiveness of your sins. And you will receive the gift of the Holy Spirit.*

Acts 2:41

> ***Those who accepted his message*** *were baptized, and about three thousand were added to their number that day.*

Acts 8:12

> *But* ***when they believed*** *Philip as he preached the good news of the kingdom of God and the name of Jesus Christ, they were baptized, both men and women.*

Those who advocate *infant baptism* point to covenantal promises that include children (Genesis 17:7) as well as instances in Scripture where entire households—including children and slaves—were baptized based on the faith of the head of the household, such as:

Acts 16:32–33

> *Then they spoke the word of the Lord to him and to all the others in his house. At that hour of the night the jailer took them and washed their wounds;* then ***immediately he and all his family were baptized.*** (See also Acts 18:8; 1 Cor. 1:16.)

Acts 2:38–39

> *Peter replied, Repent and be baptized, every one of you, in the name of Jesus Christ for the forgiveness of your sins. And you will receive the gift of the Holy Spirit.* ***The promise is for you and your children and for all who are far off***—*for all whom the Lord our God will call.*

Early Debate

Some of the earliest writings from the church fathers show that a debate over baptism for believers vs. infants was underway within the first hundred years of Christianity's beginnings.

Tertullian (AD 145–220), early church leader, contended that baptism was for believers, arguing that a conscious choice should precede baptism. On the other hand, Cyprian (AD 200–258), bishop of Carthage in North Africa, supported infant baptism, which was becoming a dominant practice in some areas.

Underlying the issue of believers' vs. infant baptism is the question of whether baptism is *primarily* about the believer personally identifying with the sacrificial death and resurrection of Christ, or whether it is *primarily* about God initiating the believer into the covenant community. (Note: Both traditions include the other view; the distinction is made to show emphasis only.) Below are descriptions of the Old Testament models upon which each tradition is based.

The Old Testament Models

Sacrifice	Circumcision
Sacrifice was a conscious act of repentance for sin.	Circumcision was the sign and seal of being initiated into God's covenant people.
• Identification with the sacrifice for sin. • Individual's conscious response to God is crucial. • The faith of the believer connects one to God, not the symbolic act alone.	• Sign and seal of initiation. • Included entire community. • Individual's faith not crucial, as symbol points to God who gives faith. • Individual, personal faith will follow God's action in covenant.

Sacrifice was a conscious act of repentance for sin and thus, only believers in the God of Israel could bring a sacrifice to the altar of God. In sacrifice, the believer was to be identified with the death of the animal given on behalf of sins. Understood in this way, baptism is seen as identification with the death of Christ (Romans 6:3–4). In both the Old Testament act of sacrifice and the New Testament act of baptism, it is faith that connects the believer to God.

Since **circumcision** was about God's command and promise in covenant relationship, it involved entire families and nations and included not only adults but also infants. The covenant ceremony included sacrifices and thus pointed to the need for cleansing and faith in God's actions on behalf of believers (Exodus 13:1–16; Leviticus 12:1–8). It also brought the individual into a covenantal relationship that made the need for sacrifice clear.

In circumcision, the immediate faith of an infant was not crucial since the effect of the symbol was to point to God who commands, promises, and gives faith in covenant relationship. Paul connected circumcision with baptism in Colossians 2:10–12: "You were circumcised with a circumcision not made with hands, ... having been buried with him in baptism." (Circumcision took place eight days after birth.)

"Wade in the Water." Postcard of a river baptism in New Bern, North Carolina, around 1900.

By looking at how the church has practiced baptism over the centuries, it is possible to understand the current variety of views about baptism.

Where Do the Differences Come From?

Growth of the Church

As the early church took root in different places in the Roman Empire, different traditions developed about baptism.

The church grew somewhat like a plant (Matthew 13:31–32). The phases of growth may be outlined in three stages:

The Early Church (around AD 1–500)	The Middle Church (around AD 500–1500)	The Modern Church (around AD 1500 to today)
Marked by • Rapid expansion similar to the rapid growth from seed to shoot seen in plants. • Time of great danger when persecutions by Roman rulers and religious authorities threatened to destroy the tender plant (Matthew 13:1–23).	• Despite early threats, the church consolidated and grew into a mature tree. • Many different peoples and cultures found a place in the church's various branches. 	• The church grew, broke open, and scattered its seeds throughout the world. • The first split took place between the Roman Catholic and Eastern Orthodox branches (AD 1054), but an even greater scattering occurred at the Reformation (c. AD 1500).

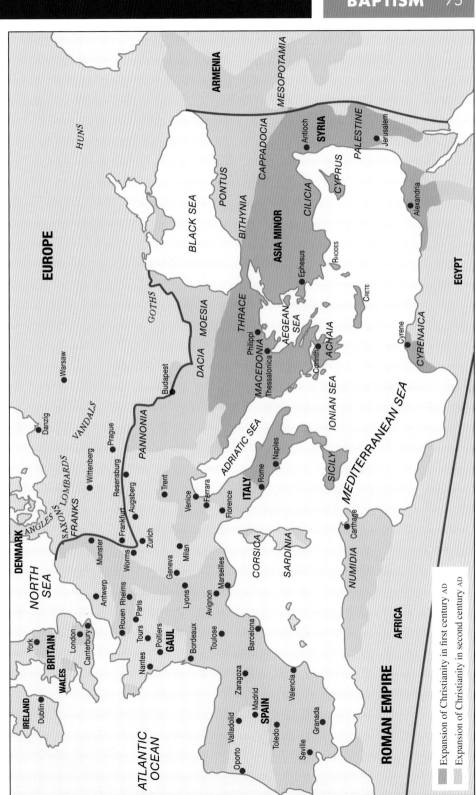

Expansion of Christianity in first century AD
Expansion of Christianity in second century AD

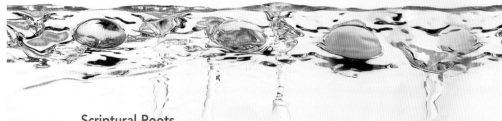

Scriptural Roots

During the growth of the church, baptism's various Scriptural roots were emphasized at different times.

Initiation: The word comes from a root meaning "to enter in." Those who are initiated into the church enter into the life of Christ's body.

"Therefore go and make disciples of all nations, baptizing them in the name of the Father and of the Son and of the Holy Spirit, and teaching them to obey everything I have commanded you. And surely I am with you always, to the very end of the age."—Matt. 28:19–20

See also: Acts 2:41; 8:12, 36–38; 1 Cor. 12:13

Identification: The word comes from a root meaning "to treat as the same." Those who are identified with Christ inherit God's riches through Christ (Ephesians 2:6–7), as children of God, because Christ identified with us by being treated as sinful.

"Or don't you know that all of us who were baptized into Christ Jesus were baptized into his death? We were therefore buried with him through baptism into death in order that, just as Christ was raised from the dead through the glory of the Father, we too may live a new life."—Romans 6:3–4

See also: Gal. 3:26–27; Col. 2:9–14; 1 Peter 3:21

One Lord, One Faith, One Baptism (Ephesians 4:4-6)

There is one body and one Spirit—just as you were called to one hope when you were called—one Lord, one faith, one baptism; one God and Father of all, who is over all and through all and in all.

The Spirit of God has an end and goal for believers—to transform us into the image of Christ (Romans 12:1–2). We may be works in progress, but we are God's work (Ephesians 2:10).

The words of the Apostle Paul in Ephesians are a humbling reminder that baptism is an external symbol of our unity as believers. Our baptism, our faith, and our Lord unite us into one body: the church.

Jesus' desire for his church is revealed in his prayer for all believers in John 17:23, "May they be brought to complete unity to let the world know that you sent me and have loved them even as you have loved me." —John 17:23b

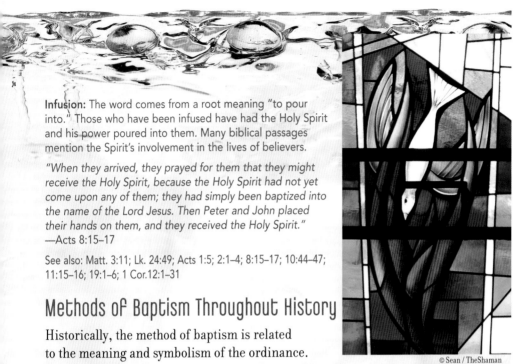

Infusion: The word comes from a root meaning "to pour into." Those who have been infused have had the Holy Spirit and his power poured into them. Many biblical passages mention the Spirit's involvement in the lives of believers.

"When they arrived, they prayed for them that they might receive the Holy Spirit, because the Holy Spirit had not yet come upon any of them; they had simply been baptized into the name of the Lord Jesus. Then Peter and John placed their hands on them, and they received the Holy Spirit."
—Acts 8:15–17

See also: Matt. 3:11; Lk. 24:49; Acts 1:5; 2:1–4; 8:15–17; 10:44–47; 11:15–16; 19:1–6; 1 Cor.12:1–31

© Sean / TheShaman

Methods of Baptism Throughout History

Historically, the method of baptism is related to the meaning and symbolism of the ordinance.

Tradition	Meaning	Mode
Initiation	• Meaning centered on the water as a sacramental symbol of God's cleansing.	• Mode of baptism is not critical; any method can be used. • The symbolic application of water is crucial. • Methods needed to be flexible during times of persecution.
Identification	• The act of immersion symbolizes identifying with Christ's death and burial, while rising out of the water symbolizes resurrection and eternal life.	• Emphasis is on outward expression of inward faith through immersion. • One of the main meanings of the Greek word *baptizo* is "to cover with water."
Infusion	• Infusion of the Spirit's power is highlighted.	• The activity of the Spirit is more important than the specific mode of baptism.

Perspectives Throughout History

	INITIATION	
The Early Church (before AD 500)	<ul><li>Baptism is a corporate act of **initiation** into the community of God.</li><li>Baptism is seen as the act and sign that the Holy Spirit is planting faith and working in the life of the new baptized. God initiates the person (1 Corinthians 12:13).</li><li>Baptism is a group act and may include clans, tribes and families, infants through adults on the model of circumcision.</li></ul>	
The Middle Church (around AD 500–1500)	<ul><li>Baptism as a corporate act of initiation becomes the dominant view.</li><li>The expansion of the church and the end of persecution pushes this majority view to the forefront as the church pursues a group identity.</li></ul>	
The Modern Church (around AD 1500 to today)	<ul><li>Baptism in this tradition is retained by the Reformed, Anglican, and Roman Catholic denominations.</li></ul>	

> **Note:**
> The act of baptism itself does not save a person. Salvation comes through Christ alone by faith (Galatians 3:26–28; Ephesians 2:8–9).

IDENTIFICATION	INFUSION
• Baptism is an individual act of faith and personal **identification** with Christ. • Baptism is seen as a personal act of faith that expresses the repentance and conversion of believers as they identify with Christ (Colossians 2:12). • Baptism is an individual act of faith and is therefore to be restricted to believers who have professed their faith.	• Baptism is God's act of **infusion** of power for ministry. • Baptism is seen as the act of receiving the Holy Spirit sent by the Father and the Son to infuse the believer with power for ministry (Acts 1:8). • Baptism is an act of both God who gives his Spirit and the believer who receives the gift of the Spirit. Only those who can make use of the gift show the evidence of the Spirit's baptism.
• Identification through baptism is minimized as churches pursue unity and consistency of teaching. • At this time, the emphasis on group identity rather than individual identity makes this view secondary.	• The infusion tradition is minimized early, becoming associated with heretical groups. • Montanism, a heresy that emphasized ecstatic prophecy, may have understood baptism in terms of infusion.
• Identification becomes the focus among Anabaptists and other Protestant bodies in the free church tradition, and the Greek Orthodox Church. • The fragmenting of the tradition of initiation in the Reformation allows for the re-emergence of the tradition of identification. • With the rise of individualism and personal choice, this view flourishes among independent church groups.	• The tradition of infusion is downplayed at the time of the Reformation, but appears intermittently. • The scattering of the church results in the tradition of infusion resurfacing slowly and sporadically. • The rise of Pentecostal and Charismatic churches (late 1800s to present) brings this view to the church. Many such groups, however, identify infusion with the "second blessing"—usually demonstrated through speaking in tongues—rather than with water baptism (Acts 8:14-17). • Other churches today believe that the Holy Spirit's power is given upon conversion or water baptism, and that believers simply need to be aware of this power from God and use it.

Baptism and Water Cleansing in the Bible

What Was John the Baptist Doing?

Is the baptism of repentance that John the Baptist practiced the same baptism that is now practiced in the church? No. However, there are several similarities:

Water is used as a symbol of purification and cleansing.	Matthew 3:5, 6, 11; 1 Peter 3:21
Repentance, turning away from the self-centered life to a God-centered one, is central.	Mark 1:4–5; Acts 2:38
The practice includes all manner of people, both genders, all levels of society.	Luke 3:7–14; Acts 16:25–33

There are also important differences between John's baptism and Christian baptism:

John's Baptism	Christian Baptism
John the Baptist and his ministry were the last of the Old Testament order.	With the coming of Christ, a new order begins (Matthew 11:7–15; John 5:33–36).
The old order is not destroyed, but becomes the basis for the new.	The new order fulfills the old but is not identical to it.
John the Baptist pointed to the coming Messianic King.	Jesus the Messiah announces the coming of the Kingdom of God.

Purification with Water in the Old Testament

- The high priest ritually washed himself before his service on the Day of Atonement, as did the priest who released the scapegoat (Leviticus 16:3, 4, 26–28).

- John the Baptist, from the priestly line of Aaron (Luke 1:5–80), may have transformed the priestly rites of purification into baptism.

- At the time of John the Baptist's preaching, some groups were practicing baptism as a ritual of purification for all believers.

- The Qumran community that produced the Dead Sea scrolls appears to have been one such community.

Baptism of Jesus by James Tissot

Baptism, Ritual and Ceremonial Cleansing in the Bible

- Baptism is connected to Old Testament practices of cleansing and purification.

- Besides meaning "to cover with water," the Greek word *baptizo* also means "to wash or dip in water."

- Old Testament people saw little distinction between physical washing and ceremonial cleanliness—physical acts were spiritual acts as well.

- Old Testament purity laws pointed toward the spiritual cleansing that was to happen through Christ.

- Thus, baptism came to symbolize the washing away of sin.

Old Testament	New Testament
Aaron–Leviticus 16:4, 24; and other priests–Leviticus 8:6; 16:26, 28; Exodus 29:4; 30:18–21; 40:12, 31, 32; Numbers 19:7–10, 19; 2 Chronicles 4:6; elders, Deuteronomy 21:6; the people, Exodus 19:10, 14.	John the Baptist–Matthew 3:5–11; 21:25; Mark 1:4–5; 11:30; Luke 3:2–3, 12; 7:29; John 1:25–33; 3:23; 10:40; Acts 1:5, 22; 10:37; 11:16; 18:25; 19:3–4
Washing with water used–For clothes, Exodus 19:10, 14; burnt offerings, Leviticus 1:9, 13; 9:14; 2 Chronicles 4:6; infants, Ezekiel 16:14; hands, Deuteronomy 21:6; Psalm 26:6; feet, Genesis 18:4.	Jesus–Matthew 3:13–16; Mark 1:8–10; Luke 3:7–8; John 3:5, 25–26; 4:1
Conditions cleansed–Leprosy, Leviticus 14:8–9; discharge of blood, Leviticus 15:1–13; defilement by dead, Leviticus 17:15–16; Numbers 19:11–13.	Disciples–John 4:2; Matthew 28:19
Common purification for normal body functions–Leviticus 12:6–8; 15:16–30.	Paul–Acts 9:18; 1 Corinthians 1:13–17
Fire and water together as symbols of purification after battle–Numbers 31:19–24.	Church–Matthew 28:19; Acts 2:38, 41; 8:12–13, 36–38; 10:46–48; 16:14–15; 18:8; 19:5; 22:16
• People in the Old Testament did not baptize. However, some practices provide the background for the New Testament baptism. Purification rites and sacrifices in the Old Testament point to the need for cleansing of impurity, evil, and sin. • In Christ, the functions of both water and blood came together. ▸ The blood of Christ cleans us from all sin and evil (1 John 1:7). ▸ The blood of Christ atones for our sins (Romans 5:9). • Baptism symbolizes this cleansing in Jesus' blood (1 Peter 3:21)	Moses, a type–1 Corinthians 10:1–2 Initiation–1 Corinthians 12:13 Identification–Romans 6:3–4; Galatians 3:27; Colossians 2:12 Infusion–Matthew 3:11,16; Mark 1:8; Luke 3:22; 24:49; John 1:32–33; 3:5; Acts 1:5; 2:1–38; 8:15–17; 10:38–47; 11:15–16; 19:2–6 Water a symbol for the cleansing by the Word and Spirit–Ephesians 5:28; Titus 3:5–6; 1 Peter 3:21

Contributing Authors: William Brent Ashby, BT; Benjamin Galan, MTS, ThM, Adjunct Professor of OT Hebrew and Literature at Fuller Seminary.

Understanding
the Book of
Revelation

Four Ways to Interpret Revelation

Symbols and Events

Key Topics and Themes

HOPE AND ENCOURAGEMENT

The book of Revelation is an exciting yet often misunderstood book of the Bible. It was probably penned between 35 and 65 years after Jesus' resurrection. This text became a source of hope and encouragement for Christians facing persecution.

This simple chart compares different ways Christians throughout the centuries have understood Revelation. Seeing the different approaches to Revelation at a glance will help clarify issues of interpretation and give new insight.

POINTS OF UNITY

Although the book of Revelation allows for many interpretations, all Christians seem to agree that:

1. The message of the book is relevant for Christians today, as it was for Christians in the times of the apostles;

2. The main purpose of the book is to provide *hope* and *encouragement* for believers of all times, especially in times of persecution or suffering;

3. The message of the book is clear on at least three points:
   - Christ is coming back and will judge humanity;
   - The powers of evil are doomed before Christ;
   - God promises a wonderful future for all who believe in Christ.

GOD ACTING IN HISTORY

Both the Old and New Testaments reveal God as Lord over history. Christians of all eras have believed that Jesus will return a second time, but not all Christians have agreed that Revelation is all about the second coming. Whether the visions in Revelation have been, are being, or have yet to be fulfilled is a matter of debate, but the spirit of the last chapter calling on Jesus to come quickly is something all Christians can agree upon—"Come, Lord Jesus!" (Revelation 22:20).

Following is a comparison of four different approaches to the book of Revelation.

Four Views	How Revelation Is Viewed	More About This View
Historicist	The book of Revelation is prophecy about church history from the time of John to the end of the world.	Historicists view the events in Revelation as symbolic descriptions of historical events throughout church history. (Some futurists also understand the Seven Churches [Revelation 1–3] in a historic manner, treating each church as descriptive of a particular era of church history.)
Preterist	The book of Revelation is prophecy that was fulfilled primarily in the first century AD.	*"Partial Preterism"* views most of Revelation as prophecy fulfilled in the first century AD, though final chapters of Revelation describe future events to occur at the end of time. *"Full Preterists"* contend that the return of Jesus described in Revelation 19 was spiritual and occurred in AD 70. Preterists are typically *amillennialists* or *postmillennialists*, though some *historic premillennialists* might fit in this category.
Futurist	Revelation is prophecy primarily about the future end of the world.	In the futurist view, all or nearly all of Revelation is yet to occur. Revelation is a prophecy that describes the end of time and the years leading immediately to the end. Dispensational premillennialists as well as some historic premillennialists interpret Revelation in this way.
Idealist	Revelation is a non-historical and non-prophetic drama about spiritual realities.	This perspective seems to have originated among ancient Alexandrian theologians, who frequently spiritualized and allegorized biblical texts, but this view also has contemporary followers.

COMPARING VIEWS

	Revelation 1:1 "soon" 1:3 "near" 1:19 "what is" (Compare, 22:6,7, 12, 20)	Revelation 2:1–3:22 The Seven Churches of Asia Minor	Revelation 4:1–3 God on His Throne	Revelation 5:1–4 The Scroll	Revelation 6:1–17 The Seals
Historical View	The prophecy began to be fulfilled close to the author's lifetime.	The prophecy begins with the seven actual churches in John's day and proceeds through history from there.	God is about to outline his rule over history: the first part of that history is revealed under the vision of the seven seals.	The scroll is the coming history of the church as God reveals it and is Lord over it.	The seals are the stages of church history, perhaps describing the church from the late first century AD to the late fourth century.
Preterist View	Near, soon, and quickly are taken literally.	The prophecy begins with the seven actual churches of Asia Minor. It then focuses on the land of Israel before AD 70.	God's courtroom in the heavenly temple is the scene. The Judge on his throne is about to hold court.	The scroll is God's bill of divorce against unfaithful Israel.	The seals describe the Roman war with the Jews which lead to the destruction of Jerusalem (AD 70).
Futurist View	These words refer to the whole of the "last days" or to the quickness with which Jesus will return.	The prophecy begins with the seven churches, which were actual churches in John's day and may also symbolize the types of churches present in the last days.	God gives John a vision from his throne of the events which are to take place "after these things."	The scroll is either the title deed to the earth or God's prophetic message in Revelation.	The seals begin to describe the great tribulation, with each opened seal leading to a greater tragedy upon the earth.
Idealist View	Christ is always at hand, near and quick to save his people.	The book begins with the seven churches, which symbolize tendencies in the church that can occur in every age.	God gives John the heavenly viewpoint of the important truths about his power over all things and his care for the church.	The scroll is God's last will and testament, revealing his salvation plan for all time.	The seals are about recurring evils throughout history and God's authority over them.

ON REVELATION

Revelation 7:1–8	Revelation 8:1–13	Revelation 9:13–19	Revelation 10:8–11
The 144,000	The Trumpets	The Four Angels at the Euphrates	The Little Scroll
The 144,000 is a symbolic number that represents the entire church.	The trumpets are the stages of church history, perhaps from about AD 400 until the fifteenth century (or to the present).	The four angels represent the four principalities of the Turkish empire. The Turks destroyed the last of the Roman empire in AD 1453.	The little scroll is the Bible at the time of the Reformation. It was sweet to those starved for God's Word, but bitter to those who wanted to control its information and keep it from common people.
The 144,000 may be the Jewish Christians who escaped the destruction of Jerusalem.	The trumpets are a vision of the Roman war with the Jews in the first century AD and extend the seals' description in further detail.	The four angels may represent the four legions of Roman soldiers stationed in Syria that Vespasian led against the Jews (around AD 70). The colors mentioned are Roman military colors.	The little scroll is the same divorce bill as in Revelation 5:1–4 but now unsealed and empty of contents, indicating that the judgments against Israel are now occurring.
The 144,000 are Jewish Christians in the last days.	The trumpets describe the events of the tribulation in the last days.	The four angels represent the armies of the Orient that will march against Israel in the last days. They will cross the Euphrates as a signal of war.	The little scroll represents the divine plan for the end of the ages, showing that the Word of God is both sweet and bitter to God's prophets and messengers.
The 144,000 are the true spiritual Israel: the church on earth.	The trumpets are about the cycles of human sin, consequences, and God's salvation.	The four angels represent the judgment of God that comes on evil when there is no more restraint, which is represented by the river Euphrates.	The little scroll is the gospel, which must and will be preached to all "peoples, nations, tongues, and kings."

Revelation	Revelation 11:1–2	Revelation 12:13–17	Revelation 13:18	Revelation 14:14–16
	The Temple	The Persecuted Woman	666	The Son of Man with the Sharp Sickle
Historical View	The measuring of the temple, the altar, and those who worship there points to God's evaluation of the church, the doctrine of justification by faith, and what constitutes true membership in the church, all of which were issues at the Reformation.	The woman is the true church under persecution. The "third of the stars" may refer to the division of the Roman Empire under three emperors in AD 313, or it may refer to post-Reformation divisions in Europe.	It may be the number of the word *Lateinos* and so refers to the Latin or Roman Catholic pope/papacy.	It is a vision of the end of the age when Christ will come and gather his own to himself.
Preterist View	The measuring of the temple and its rooms, like the eating of the scroll in chapter 10, mirror what happens in Ezekiel 40–47. Both indicate the destruction of the temple and the separation of the faithful (symbolized by the sanctuary) from the unfaithful (symbolized by the court).	The woman is faithful Israel that gave birth to Christ (the Child). The Dragon, Satan, persecuted the Messianic church, but she escaped the destruction of Jerusalem by heeding Jesus' words (Luke 21:20–22) and fleeing to the desert hills (the prepared place).	It is the number that the letters in the name "Nero Caesar" add up to.	It is a vision of the coming of Christ to gather and preserve his church from the judgment that was to befall Jerusalem.
Futurist View	The measuring of the temple refers to the nation of Israel and the temple that will be rebuilt in the last days. Israel has been restored but still awaits the rebuilding of her faith. This faith will center on the new temple and will eventually lead some Jews to faith in Christ.	The woman is Israel (sun, moon and stars, Genesis 37:9). The Child is Christ (rod of iron, Psalm 2:9). The Dragon is Satan behind the coming Antichrist. As the head of the revived "Roman Empire," the Antichrist will attack Israel.	It is the number of the future Antichrist— someone who will be like Nero back from the dead.	It is a vision of the coming harvest at the end of the age when Christ will separate the wicked for judgment.
Idealist View	The measuring of the temple and the leaving of the outer court indicates the division that has always been present between true believers and those who are Christians only in name. The trampling of the court signifies the way the unbelieving world corrupts the church, but this will only be for a short while.	The woman is Israel as the ideal symbol of all the faithful. The Child is Christ and the Dragon is Satan, the great persecutor of the Church in every age. The stars are the angels that fell with Satan at his rebellion. The seven heads and crowns speak of Satan's full political power and authority. The ten horns are military might.	It is the number of imperfection and human evil that leads to idol worship.	It is a vision of the last judgment and the coming of Christ at the end of the age.

Revelation 15:1–4	Revelation 16:10–11	Revelation 17: 1–12	Revelation 18:9–24
The Song of Moses and of the Lamb	The Fifth Bowl	The Great Prostitute	The Fall of Babylon
The song of final salvation from the slavery of the Roman Catholic religious and political power known as the papacy.	The bowl is the judgment upon the Roman Pope Pius VI that occurred when the French revolutionary forces stripped the Vatican and took the Pope captive in 1798. The Pope was forced to flee Rome again in 1848. This event was actually predicted using 1260 days as years (12:6).	The prostitute is the corrupt Roman Catholic Church, including false "Protestant" churches that have come out of her. Her political and religious influence is carried by the beastly Roman papacy and Western European culture.	The destruction of Papal Rome (Babylon) will be complete and utterly devastating. The consequences of preaching a false gospel, persecuting true believers and dabbling in power politics will bring her to this end. Many will mourn her loss but it will be final.
The song of salvation from and victory over the ungodly religious and political persecution that Christians suffered in Israel and the Roman world.	The bowl is the judgment that fell upon Rome in AD 69. In that single year, Nero committed suicide, three emperors were deposed, civil war set Roman against Roman, and the Temple of Jupiter Capitoline was burned to the ground, causing darkness during the day.	The prostitute is Jerusalem. Her political and false religious influence is carried by the Roman Empire (Beast). The seven heads are Rome and the first seven emperors, Nero (the sixth of the emperors) ruling at that time. The ten horns are the ten imperial provinces.	The destruction of Jerusalem (Babylon) is sudden and complete. The misery and the economic disaster is nearly indescribable and a source of great despair. To this day, the temple has never been rebuilt.
The song of salvation from the last-days persecution of the Antichrist and resulting judgment of God. Believers may experience some persecution but they will not have to endure God's wrath.	The bowl is the coming judgment upon the revived Roman Empire that will happen in the last days.	The prostitute is the symbol of a false religious system, a new world religious order. The religious coalition will have political influence tied to the power of the Beast (Antichrist) who is the head of the alliance (ten horns) of ten nations in Europe in the last days.	The destruction of the coming world religious, political and economic system— under the control of the Antichrist and the False Prophet—will be a crash of unparalleled dimension.
The song of salvation that all the redeemed have sung throughout history and will sing anew when Christ comes again.	The bowl shows what will happen and does happen to those who steadfastly oppose God. The judgments of darkness and sores recall the plagues of Egypt.	The prostitute is all false and corrupt religion that has allied itself with political power in order to dominate. God warns that such religion shall come to an awful end when true faith triumphs.	The destruction of Babylon reveals that God's judgment is complete and final. Whether it is Nineveh, Babylon, Rome or any other economic power that opposes God, it is destined to fail.

	Revelation 19:1–10	Revelation 20:1–15	Revelation 21:1–27	Revelation 22:1–21
Revelation	The Marriage of the Lamb and His Bride	The Millennium	The New Creation	The Salvation and Healing of the Nations
Historical View	The entire removal of false religion represented by Rome/Babylon will leave the faithful to accomplish the purpose for which Christ came—the evangelization of the rest of the world. All people will be invited to come into relationship (the marriage feast with God).	The millennium is viewed as Christ's present, spiritual reign in the lives of his people (amillennialism).	The new creation will come with Christ at his second coming, yet there is a real sense in which it has already arrived in the believer's heart. Christians live now as citizens of the New Jerusalem.	It is happening now and will finally be completed when Christ returns.
Preterist View	The entire book has been about faithfulness using the image of marriage: the divorce bill in chapter 5, the imagery of the persecuted woman and the prostitute. The book builds toward the marriage feast of Christ and his church.	In partial preterism, the millennium may be Christ's literal reign on earth (premillennialism) or a spiritual reign (postmillennialism and amillennialism). In full preterism, the millennium refers to Christ's spiritual return and reign, beginning in the first century (amillennialism).	The new creation is now and future. Since the destruction of the old Jerusalem, Christians are building the New Jerusalem here and now, wherever the gospel is believed, as well as expecting it in full when Christ returns.	It will continue as the gospel grows and spreads throughout the world. Jesus will finalize and renew all things when he comes.
Futurist View	The entire church is the bride of Christ whose marriage is announced and celebrated. This scene refers to events near the end of the world and history.	The millennium is the future, physical reign of Jesus Christ on earth (premillennialism).	The new creation will come when Christ comes again and ushers in the age to come.	It will continue until the great tribulation when the Antichrist will temporarily prevail. Christ in his second coming will triumph and usher in the final salvation and healing of all the faithful.
Idealist View	The entire sweep of sacred history may be seen through the lens of the ancient Jewish wedding tradition. The prophets announced the wedding. Jesus comes and betroths his bride (church), paying the dowry on the cross. When Jesus comes again, he will offer his bride a wedding feast.	The millennium is viewed as Christ's present, spiritual reign in the lives of his people (amillennialism).	The new creation is something God continually does with each new day. Yet there will come a day when Christ will personally return and make all things new.	It is what God has always been doing in the world—seeking and saving the lost. Christ will bring all things right when he returns.

Seven Messages to Churches
(Revelation 1:1–3:22)

INTRODUCTION (1:1–8)
Blessing 1
Vision of Christ

MESSAGES TO THE CHURCHES

1. EPHESUS
Praise: Hard work, perseverance
Criticism: Forgot first love
Exhortation: Repent
Reward: Right to eat from the tree of life

2. SMYRNA
Praise: You are rich!
Criticism: None
Exhortation: Be faithful
Reward: Not hurt by second death

3. PERGAMUM
Praise: Remain faithful
Criticism: Idolatry and sexual immorality
Exhortation: Repent
Reward: A white stone with a new name

4. THYATIRA
Praise: Deeds, love and faith, and perseverance
Criticism: Idolatry and sexual immorality
Exhortation: "Hold on to what you have until I come"
Reward: The morning star

5. SARDIS
Praise: None
Criticism: "You are dead"
Exhortation: Wake up
Reward: Be dressed in white, never blotted out from the book of life

6. PHILADELPHIA
Praise: Deeds and faithfulness
Criticism: None
Exhortation: Hold on to what you have
Reward: Become a pillar of the temple

7. LAODICEA
Praise: None
Criticism: You are lukewarm
Exhortation: Be earnest and repent
Reward: Will be seated with Christ

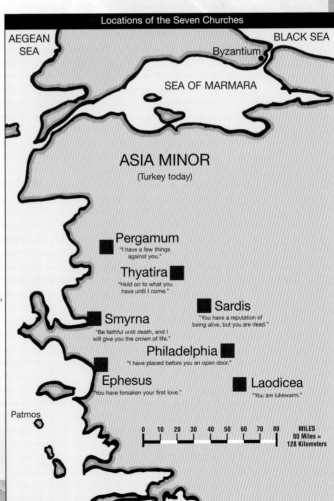

Locations of the Seven Churches

AEGEAN SEA

BLACK SEA

Byzantium

SEA OF MARMARA

ASIA MINOR
(Turkey today)

Pergamum
"I have a few things against you."

Thyatira
"Hold on to what you have until I come."

Sardis
"You have a reputation of being alive, but you are dead."

Smyrna
"Be faithful until death, and I will give you the crown of life."

Philadelphia
"I have placed before you an open door."

Ephesus
"You have forsaken your first love."

Laodicea
"You are lukewarm."

Patmos

0 10 20 30 40 50 60 70 80
MILES
80 Miles = 128 Kilometers

Seven Seals
(Revelation 4:1–8:5)

Interlude:
Vision of Heaven (4:1–11)
Scroll with Seven Seals and the Lamb
(5:1–14)

Opening of Seals (6:1–8:5)
1. **First Seal:** White Horse—*Conqueror*
2. **Second Seal:** Red Horse—*No peace*
3. **Third Seal:** Black Horse—*Famine*
4. **Fourth Seal:** Pale Horse—*Pestilence*
5. **Fifth Seal:** Martyrs under the altar
6. **Sixth Seal:** Earthquake, sun black

Interlude:
144,000 sealed (7:1–8)
The Great Multitude
(7:9–17)

7. **The Seventh Seal:**
   It contains seven angels with
   trumpets (8:1–2)
   The angel with golden censer
   (8:3–5)

Seven Trumpets
(Revelation 8:2–11:19)

1. **First Trumpet**—Hail, fire, blood

2. **Second Trumpet**—Fiery mountain
   in sea, 1/3 of sea becomes blood

3. **Third Trumpet**—star falls on 1/3
   of rivers

4. **1/3 of Sun, 1/3 Moon, 1/3 Stars**

Interlude: Woe! Woe! Woe! (8:13)

5. **Fifth Trumpet**—Demon locust
   from the Abyss

6. **Sixth Trumpet**—Two-hundred-
   million demonic riders from the
   Euphrates

Interlude (10:1–11:14):
The Little Scroll: Promise for
the church

7. **Seventh Trumpet**—"The kingdom
   of the world has become the kingdom
   of our Lord…" (11:15)

Seven Symbolic Histories
(Revelation 12:1–14:20)

The Woman and the Dragon

SYMBOLIC HISTORIES

1. HISTORY OF THE DRAGON (12:7–12)
   Defeated
   The "ancient serpent"

2. HISTORY OF THE WOMAN (12:13–17)
   Persecuted by the dragon
   Defended by God

3. THE SEA BEAST (13:1–10)
   Ten horns and seven heads
   Blasphemer
   Has power to make war

4. THE EARTH BEAST (13:11–18)
   Two horns
   Deceiver
   666—The number of the beast

5. THE 144,000 (14:1–5)
   Marked with God's name
   Worshippers

6. THE ANGELIC ANNOUNCERS (14:6–11)
   First angel: "Fear God"
   Second angel: "Fallen! Fallen is Babylon the Great"
   Third angel: Warning against the mark of the beast

7. THE HARVEST (14:14–20)

Seven Bowls
(Revelation 15:1–16:21)

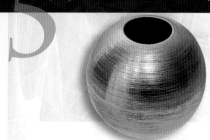

Commissioning of the Seven Angels with the Last Seven Plagues (15:1–8)

The Seven Bowls

1. **First Bowl**—Painful sores

2. **Second Bowl**—Turns sea into blood

3. **Third Bowl**—Turns rivers and springs of water into blood

4. **Fourth Bowl**—Sun burns people with fire

5. **Fifth Bowl**—Plunges kingdom of the beast into darkness

6. **Sixth Bowl**—Dries up the Euphrates; Armageddon

7. **Seventh Bowl**—Judgment against Babylon. "It is done!"

6 Seven Messages of Judgment
(Revelation 17:1–19:10)

7 Seven Visions
(Revelation 19:11–22:5)

Judgment against Babylon

Description of symbolic characters

1. **First angelic message** (17:7–18):
   Explanation of the vision

2. **Second angelic message** (18:1–3):
   Announcement of the fall
   of Babylon

3. **Third angelic message** (18:4–8):
   Call to God's people; God's
   judgment on Babylon

4. **The kings of the earth** (18:9–10):
   Lament for the fall of Babylon

5. **The merchants of the earth** (18:11–17):
   Lament for the fall of Babylon

6. **The seafaring people** (18:18–19)
   Lament for the fall of Babylon
   Rejoice for God's judgment (18:20)

7. **Seventh angelic message** (18:21–24)
   Announcement of the final
   destruction of Babylon

1. **First Vision** (19:11–16)
   Heaven opens and the white horse
   rider appears

2. **Second Vision** (19:17–18)
   Angel invites birds to "the great
   supper of God"

3. **Third Vision** (19:19–21)
   The beast and kings ready for war

4. **Fourth Vision** (20:1–3)
   The thousand years (millennium)

5. **Fifth Vision** (20:4–10)
   Thrones with judges and
   Satan's doom

6. **Sixth Vision** (20:11–15)
   Judgment of the dead

7. **Seventh Vision** (21:1–22:5)
   A vision of "a new heaven and
   a new earth."

Epilogue (22:6–21)

*Jesus is coming back: "Amen. Come,
Lord Jesus."*

TERMS IN THE BOOK OF REVELATION

666—Number of the beast, spelled out in Rev. 13:18 as *six hundred sixty-six*. Greek and Hebrew did not have written numbers. Instead, either they spelled out the number, or they wrote out the number using the letters in the alphabet. For example, the first letter of the alphabet might represent the number one, and so on. Many scholars point out that, in Hebrew, the number of Nero's name can be 666 if written using *Neron*, the Latin spelling of the name. (Nero reigned AD 54–68. He was the first emperor to engage in specific persecution of Christians.) A good approach to this issue is to remember that six is a symbol of incompletion; 666 indicated total imperfection.

144,000—Group of believers who endure the great tribulation (Rev. 7:14). Some believe that these persons are literally 144,000 Jews—12,000 from each tribe—who embrace Jesus Christ as their Lord (see Rev. 7:4–9). Others suggest that the terms "Israel" and "twelve tribes" often refer to Christians (Rom. 9:6–8; Gal. 6:16; James 1:1). Therefore, the number would point to God's people (symbolized by twelve tribes, twelve apostles, or both) multiplied by 1,000 (a number that symbolizes an extreme multitude or length of time)—in other words, the full number of those who belong to God.

Abomination of desolation—An event that desecrates the temple in Jerusalem and is a signal to Jesus' followers that soon Jerusalem will be ruined. Mentioned in Matthew 24:15, it may refer to the destruction of the temple in AD 70 by the Romans, or Roman plans to set up a statue of the Emperor in the temple in AD 40, or some future event.

Antichrist—(from Greek, *antichristos*, in place of Christ) Anyone who denies what the apostles taught about Jesus Christ (1 John 2:18–22; 4:3; 2 John 1:7). Specifically, the antichrist is a Satanic counterfeit of Jesus Christ, described as "lawless" and as a "beast" (2 Thessalonians 2:3–8; Revelation 13:1–18; 17:3–17). The antichrist could be a specific person who rises to power during a time of tribulation or a symbol of false teachers and leaders who will arise when the end of the age draws near.

Armageddon—(from Hebrew, *Har-Megiddo*, Mount Megiddo) The city of Megiddo was located between the Plain of Jezreel and Israel's western coast. Deborah, Gideon, Saul, Ahaziah, and Josiah fought decisive battles near Megiddo—largely

because the area around Megiddo is broad and flat. So the valley of Megiddo became the symbol of a point of decisive conflict. Some believe that a literal battle will occur near Megiddo near the end of time. Others view the reference to Armageddon as a symbol of an ultimate conflict between spiritual forces of good and evil.

Babylon—Revelation 17 presents the figure of a prostitute called Babylon riding upon a scarlet beast. The name is symbolic, yet interpretations vary:

1. Jerusalem: Jewish people assisted the Romans in their persecution of Christians after AD 64. The fall of Babylon could be a symbolic reference to the fall of Jerusalem in AD 70.

2. Rome: After AD 70, Jewish writers often referred to Rome as "Babylon."[1] The name may symbolize the political and religious powers in every age that attempt to defy God and to persecute his people.

3. One-world government and religion: Babylon may be a reference to a one-world government and one-world religion that will emerge near the end of time.

Beasts, two—Symbolic creatures described in Revelation 11:7 and 13:1–18.

The first beast: This creature rises from the sea and has ten horns and seven heads. The seven heads seem to point to Rome, the city known for its seven hills. Some interpreters understand this reference to Rome as a literal reference to a power that will arise from Rome near the end of time; others view it as a symbolic reference to the powers in every age that defy God's dominion and persecute God's people. The beast claims blasphemous names for itself—much like Domitian, emperor from AD 81 until 96, who demanded that he be addressed as "Lord and God." One of the horns seemed to have died but then returned to life—much like the false rumor that emerged after the death of Nero that he had come back to life.[2]

The second beast: This creature rises from the earth with horns like a lamb and a voice like a dragon—in other words, a satanic parody of Jesus Christ, the Lamb of God. Some interpreters understand this creature as a literal leader who will encourage people to worship the first beast. Others view the second beast as a symbol of any religion in any time period that focuses worshipers on anything other than Jesus Christ.

TERMS IN THE BOOK OF REVELATION

Final judgment—The event described in Rev. 20:11-15, when God resurrects all people, judges them from the great white throne, and delivers them to their eternal destinies.

Letters to the Seven Churches—After the opening vision (Chapter 1), John begins to write to the messengers (angels) of seven churches, Ephesus, Smyrna, Pergamum, Thyatira, Sardis, Philadelphia, and Laodicea. The messages review the churches' histories, give warnings and commands, and tells them to prepare for what is about to unfold. Scholars agree that these were actual messages to real churches in existence in John's day, though some see in the seven churches patterns that apply to the church in specific past, present, or future eras.

Mark of the beast—Indication of a person's allegiance to the teachings of the antichrist (Revelation 13:16–17). The people of God receive a similar mark, indicating their loyalty to Jesus (Revelation 7:3; 9:4; 14:1; 22:4). Some biblical students believe that the mark of the beast will be an actual mark, required by the antichrist. (Between the Old and New Testaments, some Jews were forced to be branded with the symbol of the god Dionysius.[3]) Other interpreters of Revelation understand the mark as a reference to someone's actions ("hand") and beliefs ("forehead"). "Hand" and "forehead" seem to carry this symbolic meaning in Exodus 13:9, 16.

Views of the Millennium—Chapter 20, the only direct reference in the Bible to a reign of Christ that lasts 1,000 years, is one of the most controversial sections of the Bible.

There are three basic views—Premillennialism, Amillennialism and Postmillennialism—that help to categorize the different interpretations.

• **Premillennialism** holds that Christ will return before the millennium. Jesus will rule the world and begin an age of peace and security. There are two varieties within this view: Historic Premillennialism and Dispensational Premillennialism.

   • *Historic Premillennialism* sees Christ's return at the end of the great tribulation. This time of tribulation may last seven years, or "seven" may symbolically refer to the completeness of this tribulation. The church will go through this time of trouble but endure to greet Christ when he comes.

   • *Dispensational Premillennialism* holds that the church will not endure the great tribulation. Christ will remove the church before that time or, alternatively, at some point before the worst experiences of the tribulation.

• **Amillennialism** is the view that the millennium is not a literal one thousand years. It refers to the period now in progress in which the gospel is spreading throughout the world and Christ is ruling at the right hand of God the Father.

• **Postmillennialism** asserts that there will be a period of great peace and security when the gospel has spread throughout the world and Christ reigns spiritually, through His people. After this time of one thousand years or so, Christ will return to end history.

Witnesses, two—Two beings described in Rev. 11:1–14 who speak the truth about God before being killed and then resurrected. (1) Some believe that these two witnesses are two people who will appear during the tribulation, near the end of time. (2) Others view them as two biblical prophets—perhaps Moses and Elijah—that have been resurrected to proclaim God's truth during the tribulation. (3) Others see the two witnesses as symbols of the Law and the Prophets—both of these testified about Jesus and yet, this testimony was rejected, even to the point of killing those that appealed to this testimony (for example, Stephen in Acts 7). If so, the "resurrection" of the two witnesses would point to a time of final vindication, a point at which God demonstrates that the Law and Prophets did indeed testify about Jesus Christ.

[1] G. K. Beale, *The Book of Revelation* (Grand Rapids, Mi: Eerdmans, 1999), 19.
[2] G. E. Ladd, *A Commentary on the Revelation of John* (Grand Rapids: MI, Eerdmans, 1972), 178–179.
[3] 3 Maccabees 2:29.

Contributing Authors: William Brent Ashby, BT; Benjamin Galan, MTS, ThM, Adjunct Professor of OT Hebrew and Literature at Fuller Seminary.

What's So Great about
Heaven

Biblical View of Heaven

Renewed Heaven and Earth

Hope for the Future

Why is heaven important?

Heaven is more than just hope for a better future. It is at the heart of God's plan for all creation. It is also at the center of the human heart.

The common experience of losing loved ones, and the eventual loss of our own lives, make the issue of heaven one with which everyone must wrestle. We wonder what happens when we die, when our loved ones die. Have we lost them forever? Are they in a better place? Will we see them again someday? What is life after death like? What is heaven like? Can we even know something about heaven?

Heaven is a source of hope, guidance, and meaning for every believer. Heaven gives:

- Hope for our future destination and strength for life in the present
- Guidance for living as God's people today
- Meaning by giving us the certainty that there is more to life than this world

In the following pages, we will answer some of the most common questions about heaven. We will also broaden our perspective about heaven. We will realize that heaven is not only about *hope* but also about *faith* and *love*.

© PHOTOCREO Michal Bednarek

What do we mean by heaven?

In popular culture, and for many believers, heaven evokes images of cloudy, ghost-like existence, or angelic beings floating about among the clouds. This image comes directly from the radical separation of the physical and spiritual worlds. Some of the misconceptions are:

Popular View of Heaven

- A place for disembodied, ghost-like beings
- A place where people sing all the time
- A place up by the clouds
- A place everyone goes after death
- A place where all beings live as angels

Biblical View of Heaven

However, the final destination of believers is not an ethereal place like that. The final destination of all believers is *the renewed heavens and earth* anticipated in Revelation 21. A very physical, concrete future awaits us when Christ comes back.

What can we know about heaven?

The answer is not as much as we would like; however, we can know just enough to be confident that:

- We can trust in God's promises.
- We will be with God and our loved ones.
- God will do something awesome with his creation.

How do we know anything about heaven?

- The only completely valid source of knowledge about heaven is the Bible. The Bible has direct and indirect information about heaven—over 600 verses in the Bible mention *heaven*.
- The Bible is the rule with which we can decide if other information is valid.
- However, for the most part, people's ideas about heaven come mainly from literature, movies, and television. Media has shaped much of our imagination and knowledge about heaven. Not all of this knowledge is accurate.
- A non-biblical understanding of the world has informed much of what popular culture knows about heaven.
- It mainly portrays heaven as boring and unappealing.

A non-biblical understanding of the universe

Behind the cloudy, ethereal idea of heaven lies the old Gnostic belief that the physical world is evil and the spiritual is good. Thus, one must focus on the spiritual to escape this evil world. This is not a biblical idea. It ignores some basic biblical facts:

A biblical understanding of the universe

1. God made the whole universe and called it *very good* (Gen. 1:31).

2. Satan is a spiritual being and is evil—thus, not all *spiritual* is good and not all *physical* is evil.

3. God promises a renewed heavens and earth at the end of time (Rev. 21).

Although sin has profoundly affected creation, God never called creation evil. It is under a curse. However, Jesus came to lift that curse and turn it into blessing. God is redeeming all of creation. At the end of time, God will renew all things to their original intention.

Understanding God's original plan for his creation helps us understand our final destination as well.

What was God's original intent for creation?

God created the whole universe for his own glory and relationships. He intended all his creatures to relate to each other, to nature, and to himself in harmony. Humanity's main and great goal in life is to glorify God (Isa. 60:21; 1 Cor. 6:20; 10:31) and enjoy him forever (Phil. 4:4; Rev. 21:3–4).

Human sin twisted God's original intentions. However, because of God's grace and faithfulness, his plans would not be frustrated. He planned to rescue his creation from the effects of sin (Rom. 8:18–27). Through the saving work of Jesus on the cross, people can find peace with God and each other. Through the same process, believers can begin the reconciliation with one another and nature.

Neos and Kainos

Greek has two different words for the idea of *new*. *Neos* is a newness of time; *kainos* is a newness of quality. A *neos* object would mean that the object did not exist and now is there. A *kainos* object means that the object was there but its quality has changed: it is better, it is made different. In this sense, the *new heavens and earth* in Rev. 21:1 are not *neos* but *kainos*. That is, God will renew, transform, improve, and refresh his creation. It will be a *kainos* heaven and earth.

What is the renewed heaven and earth?

© Andrejs Pidjass

This process will have a glorious ending when Christ returns. He will renew all things (Rev. 21:1). It will not be a different creation or a non-creation. It will be *this* creation renewed; God will restore his creation to its original glory and purpose. As if to close the circle, what God began at Eden he will fulfill in Revelation. Not everything will be the same. Some things from the biblical idea of Eden will continue in the renewed creation; others will end.

We do have glimpses of heaven, even if many things are not clear. We can see it in the love we experience for and from people, in the majesty of nature's beauty and power, in the generosity and kindness of people in times of need, in the smile of a happy baby, in the loyalty and warmth of our pets, in the tenderness and wisdom of old age, and in moments of deep emotional and spiritual connections with our loved ones and God.

What is our hope for the future?

Our hope for the future is firmly rooted in God's faithfulness. We can trust that God will do what he has promised us because he has been faithful in the past. We can safely conclude that many features and characteristics of this world will continue in the renewed creation. Of course, there will be things that will end as well. Based on biblical testimony, we can identify many things that will continue and some that will not.

© Monkey Business Images

What Will Continue	What Will End

• Physical bodies
• Emotions (relationships)
• Nature
    Daily cycles
    Weather
    Animals—including pets
• Many activities, such as:
    Work (Gen. 2:15)
    Learning (1 Cor. 13:12)
    Science
    Art (Rev. 14:2–3)
    Entertainment
	• No evil
	• No curse
	• No brokenness, emotional or physical
	• No more sin
	• No death
	• No marriage
	• No more suffering or sadness
	• No war
	• No famine
	• No need for temples

"This is the will of Him who sent Me, that of all that He has given Me I lose nothing, but raise it up on the last day." —John 6:39 (*NASB*)

Besides referring to people, this text also refers to God's creation. The neuter pronoun *it* (Greek *auto*) would seem to extend Jesus' mission from people to all of creation (see Romans 8:19–22 and Colossians 1:20). Jesus' words in John 6:39 are a guarantee that no good thing shall be lost, but rather shall have some new and fulfilled form in the renewed creation. Everything good belongs to Christ, who is the life of the whole world as well as the life of every believer (John 6:33, 40). All things good in this world will continue to exist in the next, but they will be transformed and improved in the renewed creation.

Why does Jesus' resurrection matter?

Jesus' resurrection gives us a good idea of what heaven may look like. The Apostle Paul makes it clear that our future is tied to Jesus' own resurrection (1 Cor. 15:12–34). He concludes, "And if Christ has not been raised, your faith is futile…" (15:17).

- Because Christ has been raised from the dead, our hope is true and secured.
- Christ is the firstfruits or first example of all who will be raised into new life (15:20).
- Our future includes a *resurrected body*; that is, it will be a physical reality. Our future resurrected bodies will be like Jesus' own resurrected body (1 Cor. 15:42–49).
- The women and the disciples recognized Jesus after his resurrection (Matt. 28:9, 17).
- Jesus' body was physical (Lk. 24:39). Jesus ate with his disciples (Lk. 24:41–43). Yet, it was not a body like ours. The Apostle Paul uses two ways to explain this difference:

1 Just as different animals have bodies suited for their environment (for the sea, the air, and the ground), so our resurrected bodies will be suited for the renewed creation (1 Cor. 15:39).

2 There are also "natural bodies" and "spiritual bodies." Both Jesus' pre- and post-Resurrection bodies were physical; the difference is about perishability. That is, natural bodies die; spiritual bodies do not. Sin has polluted and damaged our natural bodies; our bodies die, decay, and are unfit for a future in God's presence. Just as God will renew this creation, also marred by sin, God will give us renewed bodies that will not be polluted by sin, will not decay, and will be fit to be in the presence of God.

© R. Gino Santa Maria

Natural Bodies	Spiritual Bodies
Psychikos	*Pneumatikos*
Derived from *psyche*, meaning "soul"	Derived from *pneuma*, meaning "spirit"

The ending *ikos* is used in Greek to make an adjective, and it means "in reference to." It does not describe the material out of which something is made. Rather, it refers to the force that animates an object. In this case, *psychikos* refers to the human soul that animates our bodies. In the case of *pneumatikos*, it refers to the Spirit, God's Spirit, as the animating force (see, for example, Rom. 1:11 and Gal. 6:1). Thus, both kinds of bodies are physical. The difference is that a "natural body" dies and a "spiritual body" does not die.

Will we be able to recognize our loved ones in heaven?

Yes! When Jesus rose from the dead and appeared to his friends and disciples, they recognized him (Luke 24:39; John 20:27). There will be continuity between our bodies today and our resurrected bodies in the renewed creation.

© Tiffany Chan

> *I know that my Redeemer lives, and that in the end he will stand upon the earth. And after my skin has been destroyed, yet in my flesh I will see God; I myself will see him with my own eyes—I, and not another. How my heart yearns within me!*
>
> —Job 19:25–27

© Monkey Business Images

What kinds of relationships will exist in heaven?

Emotions and relationships are a very important part of what it means to be human. There will be emotions and relationships in heaven, though they may not be exactly the same. They will be renewed emotions, as they were meant to be from the beginning: joyful, satisfying, enriching, intimate, and refreshing.

There will be no sorrow, or regrets, or guilt. Rather, love, compassion, gentleness, tenderness, and other emotions will find new heights and depths in heaven. Relationships will be all we can imagine and more.

Will there be disabilities, injuries or deformities in heaven?

© Florin C

No. There will be no brokenness at all, either emotional or physical. God will renew our bodies; they will be beautiful and work as God intended them to. Because Jesus' injuries were present after his resurrection (Luke 24:39; John 20:27), many people think that martyrs, those who died for the name of Jesus, will wear their healed scars as badges of honor. Although it is possible, it remains, like so many other things about heaven, just speculation.

Will our bodies need food, clothing, and language in heaven?

Because we do not understand the nature of the future bodies, it is difficult to know whether they will need food, clothing, and languages. However, since our bodies will preserve much of their characteristics, we could imagine that language, food, and clothing will have very similar functions. The beautiful diversity of characters and gifts makes life more interesting. Each person reflects God's image in a way that none other can. Together, with our differences and similarities, with our talents and strengths, we reflect God's image as no individual human could.

Yet, there will certainly be differences as well. Now, differences in culture and expression can be causes of deep, fierce divisions (Gen. 11:1–9). However, in the renewed creation, communication will be transparent. We will say what we mean, and people will fully understand us. This side of heaven, clothing can be used as a status symbol that can serve our pride. It is also used to cover our shame. There will be no shame in the renewed creation, nor will we have the need to boost our ego at the expense of others. Rather, clothing will not conceal but could reveal our inner being.

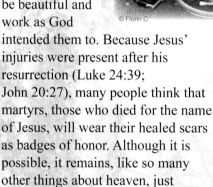

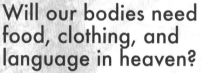

© Monkey Business Images

Will heaven be boring?

Definitely not! People may get the idea that heaven will be boring because we will worship God all day long in heaven. It is true—we will worship God non-stop! But let's revisit what we mean by *worship*.

Worship is not just the singing and praying part of Christian church services. Everything we do can be worship: from the moment we wake up, take our meals, relate to others, do our work, play games, and live life. Worship is not just an activity; it is primarily an attitude. Worship is the attitude that arises when we recognize who God is and who we are:

God	Human
He is the creator	We are the creatures
He is in control of our lives	We depend completely on God's grace and mercy
He is all powerful	We are limited and weak
He knows all things	We know imperfectly
He loves us unconditionally	We are just learning to love in the same way

Worship is the attitude that acknowledges God's presence at every moment in our daily lives, sometimes moving us to tears, sometimes to great joy, to repentance, to humility, to gratitude, to hard work, to commitment, to compassion, to love.

In the busyness of our lives, we often miss this reality: God is interested and active in our lives! We may go days or weeks without realizing that our words, actions, and thoughts have brought glory or sadness to God. This forgetfulness will find no place in the renewed creation; we will not miss God in our lives because he will dwell in our midst.

Worship = an attitude of awe and gratitude, of humble submission to God's greatness and grace, of obedience and love.

© Donald Linscott

What will we do in heaven?

The Bible does not give many details about activities in heaven. But we can be sure that:

- God loves his creation. He proclaimed it good (Gen. 1:31).
- Nature itself reflects God's greatness and glory (Ps. 19).
- Nature will be renewed so it may fulfill God's purposes.

So it is at least possible that much of the new creation will be similar to what we experience now. The best things about this world will just become better in the renewed creation.

Will we have pets?

Our relationships with our pets are also important and meaningful. These relationships reflect the way God intended us to relate to animals in general: with love, respect, and companionship. Will God, then, resurrect our beloved pets? Yes, it is perfectly possible. We cannot be sure, since the Bible does not address this issue, but based on God's love for animals, their role as our companions, it is at least possible.

© Quincy Dein

The wolf and the lamb will feed together, and the lion will eat straw like the ox, but dust will be the serpent's food. They will neither harm nor destroy on all my holy mountain.

—Isaiah 65:25

Will there be work?

Because work can become an almost painful toil, we often wonder if *rest* means no more working. But remember that

- Work is also a form of worship;

- God meant for humans to help take care of his creation (Gen. 2:15).

Each person will develop and thrive with his or her own talents. We will no longer work in places that do not allow us to grow as individuals, or where our work might be unappreciated, or where we cannot possibly be happy.

God intended work to be a joyful activity. Rather than just making a living, work should be a way to fellowship with God by caring for his world. For this reason, we can be sure we will have plenty of interesting things to do in the renewed creation!

Will there be learning, science, sports, and arts?

As with work, we could imagine the same for learning, science, arts, and sports. The gifts and talents of painters, poets, athletes and scientists will be used simply to worship God.

> *Whatever you do, work at it with all your heart, as working for the Lord, not for men, since you know that you will receive an inheritance from the Lord as a reward. It is the Lord Christ you are serving.*
> —Colossians 3:23–24

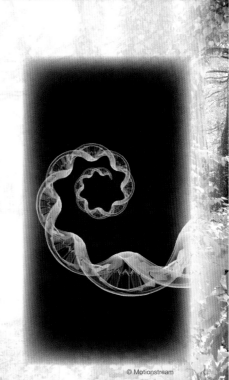
© Motionstream

© Lilun

What's so great about heaven?

Everything! Heaven is all we ever dreamt and more. In this life, we grow, reach our peak, and begin a slow descent until our life ends. Life in the intermediate heaven will be much better because we will be in God's presence. However, life in the renewed creation will be beyond our imagination.

It is true that we do not know many facts about the renewed creation, heaven, and even less about the intermediate state, intermediate heaven. However, what we read in the Bible and what we know about God give us great hope and joy.

> *Dear friends, now we are children of God, and what we will be has not yet been made known. But we know that when he appears, we shall be like him, for we shall see him as he is. Everyone who has this hope in him purifies himself, just as he is pure.*
> —1 John 3:2–3

The Ultimate Great Escape?

- Heaven is not an escapist idea.
- We do not think about heaven to escape this world's troubles—we think about heaven as a guide to live better in this world, to serve God with greater joy, and to show others God's great love.
- For many believers who suffer persecution for their faithfulness, and others who suffer in this life in indescribable ways, heaven is a great source of comfort.

- Knowing that God will make all things right one day gives us strength to continue life in faithfulness and obedience.

Who will be in heaven and how do we get there?

- In popular culture, it's common to believe that all people go to heaven, and, in some cases, they become angels. However, biblical testimony does not support either of these ideas.

- Just as we acknowledge the reality of heaven, we must recognize the reality of hell. We don't know very much about hell either, except that it exists, it is a place of punishment, and there is only one way to escape it. The other details are hidden from us.

- The Bible is clear, however, to specify who will go to heaven. Only those who have surrendered their lives to Jesus and who experience the renewal of their hearts will be allowed in God's presence.

© David Huntley

> *For God so loved the world that he gave his one and only Son, that whoever believes in him shall not perish but have eternal life. For God did not send his Son into the world to condemn the world, but to save the world through him.*
> —John 3:16–17

What is the New Jerusalem?

The book of Revelation provides another image of the renewed creation: the city of Jerusalem (Rev. 21:2). The city is described as a bride and its dimensions are detailed. Believers understand this text in different ways. Some understand the city to be a literal city, and the dimension an accurate representation of what the city will be like. The resulting picture is an enormous cube of about 1,400 miles per side.

Others take this image as a symbolic representation of God's people. Since the image of the bride ready to marry the Lamb occurs before, and it seems applied to God's people (Rev. 19:7), it is possible that the Holy City stands for God's holy people. It is perfectly possible that there will be no seas (21:1), or sun and moon (21:23). It is also possible that the language is symbolic—it says the "city does not need the sun or the moon…" not that they will not exist. If there is continuity between this creation and the renewed creation, as we have suggested, then the beauty of the sun and the moon will be present, even if not needed.

In any case, it is clear that:

- The renewed creation is God's work, since it comes from above.
- It is large enough to fit all of God's people and more.
- It points at the beauty and splendor of the renewed creation.
- God dwells in its midst.
- It closes the circle from Paradise in the Garden of Eden to the Holy City in the new heavens and new earth.

Original Creation (Genesis)	*Renewed Creation (Revelation)*
Heaven and earth created, 1:1	Heavens and earth renewed, 21:1
Sun created, 1:16	No need of sun, 21:23
The night established, 1:5	No night there, 22:5
The seas created, 1:10	No more seas, 21:1
The curse enters the world, 3:14–17	No more curse, 22:3
Death enters the world, 2:19	Death is no more, 21:4
Humanity is cast out of paradise, 3:24	Humanity is restored to paradise, 22:14
Sorrow and pain begin, 3:17	Sorrow, tears, and pain end, 21:4

Regarding knowledge of heaven, we must humbly recognize our limits.

The secret things belong to the Lord our God, but the things revealed belong to us and to our children forever. —Deuteronomy 29:29

- Mystery requires faith to know that God is in control.
- We do not need to know everything.
- We know all that we need to be faithful and obedient.

What happens when people die?

When one experiences the loss of a loved one, the pain of the loss makes it difficult to focus on the ultimate destination. The immediate concern is *what has happened to my loved one? Is my loved one in heaven?*

What will happen to me when I die?

Although some of the details remain hidden, we know that:

- Our life and future are secure in God's hands (Ps. 34:6; 91:4; Is. 25:4; Rom. 8:37–39).

- We go to a place of waiting in the presence of God (1 John 3:2–3). Many theologians call this period between our deaths and Jesus' return the *intermediate state*.

- It is not a permanent place; the whole creation waits for the final redemption at the end of time.

- It is not a place up by the clouds; we do not know where it is, but it is where Jesus is present.

Can we be sure what happens after we die? **Yes!**

- Believers will enjoy the blessing of God's presence (1 John 3:2–3; Rev. 21:22).

- Believers from all of history wait in joy and peace, but with longing, for the return of Christ (Rev. 6:9–10).

- As believers, we will join them at some point.

- When God renews all things, we will all dwell together in the new heavens and the new earth (Rev. 21–22).

Author: Benjamin Galan, MTS, ThM, Adjunct Professor of OT Hebrew and Literature at Fuller Seminary

© Jerry Zitterman

Rose Bible Basics:

What Christians Believe at a Glance

A FREE downloadable version of this guide is available at rose-publishing.com. Click on "News & Info," then on "Downloads."

The **leader guide** covers each chapter of this book and includes teaching tips, additional resources, and answer keys for the study guide worksheets.

The **study guide** includes reproducible worksheets and/or discussion questions for each chapter.

What participants will gain from this study:
- Identify key Christian beliefs.
- Know why the creeds are important for understanding the essentials of Christianity.
- Be able to answer important questions about who Jesus is.
- Be able to correct misunderstandings about the Trinity and the deity of Jesus.
- Learn the differences and similarities between 12 major denominations.
- Understand why and how Christians are baptized.
- Compare four different ways that Christians view the book of Revelation.
- Learn what the Bible teaches about heaven.

© 2010 Rose Publishing. www-rose-publishing.com. Permission granted to reproduce for classroom use only. Taken from Rose Bible Basics: What Christians Believe #772X ISBN:9781596364141

LEADER GUIDE

Spend time in prayer before each session and pray for each participant.

CHAPTER 1: ESSENTIAL DOCTRINE MADE EASY

Main Idea

These essential doctrines unify Christians who seek to have a biblical faith, though Christians may not agree on how they work out the details of their faith.

Teaching Tips

Introduce participants to the purposes of this study. Ask them what they hope to gain from the study or why they joined this study.

Ask participants to share about their own religious background. This will help you better plan the following sessions to meet the needs of the group.

Clarify with participants that these essential doctrines are what must be *true* for salvation to be possible, not that all these must be *believed* for a person to be saved (see "To Believe or Not to Believe?" section). Be careful to avoid communicating to participants that they might not be saved because they don't quite understand or have doubts about some of these doctrines.

Digging Deeper

This We Believe by Gen. Eds. John N. Akers, John H. Armstrong, and John D. Woodbridge (Zondervan, 2000); Each chapter is written by well-known Christians to explain the basic principles of Christianity.

To prepare for this session use a systematic theology handbook to look up theological terms or concepts that you are not familiar with. See for example: *Systematic Theology: An Introduction to Biblical Doctrine* by Wayne Grudem (Zondervan, 1994); *Introducing Christian Doctrine 2ⁿᵈ Ed.* by Millard Erickson (Baker, 2001).

Also see the resources listed at the end of the chapter.

Worksheet Key

(1) God (2) Persons (3) good works (or deeds) (4) human being (5) perfect (or sinless) (6) God (or divine) (7) human (8) rescue (or save) (9) works (or deeds) (10) death (11) bodily (12) Jesus / Christ (13) represents (or mediates/intercedes for) (14) coming

CHAPTER 2: CREEDS AND HERESIES: THEN & NOW

Main Idea

Creeds help us distinguish between essential and nonessential Christian beliefs.

Teaching Tips

If you are unsure of how to pronounce some of the terms in this chapter, before the session, go to Dictionary.com (http://dictionary.reference.com/). This website has on-screen and audio pronunciation guides for most of the terms used in this chapter.

Close the session by reading the Apostles' Creed aloud together. Print out the creed for each participant or put the creed on a screen for participants to follow along.

© 2010 Rose Publishing. www.rose-publishing.com. Permission granted to reproduce for classroom use only. Taken from Rose Bible Basics: What Christians Believe #772X ISBN:9781596364141

Digging Deeper

Creeds of Christendom, vol. 1-II and *Creeds of the Evangelical Protestant Church* by Philip
   Schaff. Classic work, accessible, and comprehensive; Can be read for free online at
   www.ccel.org/index/author-S.html

Heresies and How to Avoid Them by Ben Quash and Michael Ward, editors. (Peabody
   Hendrickson, 2007)

"Historic Creeds and Confessions" by Rick Brennan at www.ccel.org/ccel/brannan/hstcrcon.html

Worksheet Key

(1) d   (2) c   (3) d   (4) False   (5) True

CHAPTER 3: THE TRINITY

Main Idea

There is only one God, and this God exists as one essence in three persons: Father, Son, and
   Holy Spirit.

Teaching Tips

This chapter jumps right into the discussion of what Christians believe about the Trinity.
   However, it might be useful to begin the session by discussing: (1) Why is believing in
   the Trinity important? (2) How does belief in the Trinity make a difference in a Christians
   spiritual life? Then move the teaching time into a discussion about the definition and
   scriptural basis of the Trinity.

The worksheet activity provided for this chapter may take considerable time so plan your
   session accordingly. This activity can be done at the beginning or middle of the session.

Digging Deeper

For further study, see the resources listed at the end of the chapter.

Worksheet

If the class is large enough, break them into three smaller groups. Assign each group a different
   list of verses from the three sections of worksheet. If the class is small, have all participants
   complete the worksheet together. When the groups complete their portion of the worksheet,
   list all the attributes and activities they found from the Scriptures onto a whiteboard or easel
   pad. Ask participants: What similar attributes and activities do you notice across all three:
   Father, Son, and Holy Spirit? Remember, this activity is not a competition. It encourages
   participants to interpret Scripture themselves, and to see how the Bible teaches the doctrine
   of the Trinity using a variety of passages taken together, rather than just all in one verse.

CHAPTER 4: LIFE OF JESUS

Main Idea

Jesus is the Christ and the Son of God. He came to save the world and made that salvation
   possible through his death and resurrection.

© 2010 Rose Publishing. www-rose-publishing.com. Permission granted to reproduce for classroom use
only. Taken from Rose Bible Basics: What Christians Believe #772X   ISBN:9781596364141

Teaching Tips

Open this session by having participants brainstorm all the words they think of when they hear the name *Jesus*. Write all the words on a whiteboard or easel pad. Identify which themes you see emerging. Explain that as Christians we are to become like Jesus, so how we view him affects how we live our lives.

Digging Deeper

Names of Jesus pamphlet (Rose Publishing). Explores who Jesus is through what his names and titles reveal.

100 Prophecies Fulfilled by Jesus (Rose Publishing). Shows how Jesus is the Messiah anticipated in the Old Testament.

Evidence for Jesus: Discover the Facts that Prove the Truth of the Bible by Ralph Muncaster (Harvest House, 2004).

Worksheet Key

(1) False (2) e (3) d (4) False (5) c

CHAPTERS 5: DENOMINATIONS COMPARISON

Main Idea

Christians are unified in several core beliefs, however there is much diversity in the specifics of other beliefs and practices.

Teaching Tips

This chapter does not cover in detail the history of each denomination. You can use this activity to explore briefly the background of each denomination. Use the resources listed below to write a short "How did this denomination begin?" paragraph for each denomination. Print each paragraph on one side of a piece of paper and on the other side print a picture representing the denomination. Hand out the papers, one to each participant, and have them read the paragraph to the group while showing the picture on the reverse side of the paper. If participant attendance is consistent, you can assign one denomination to each participant at the end of the previous session. Then each participant can come back this session and share with the group what they found out about the roots of that denomination.

This chapter is packed with facts and information, so be sure to allow time for discussing the practical aspects of this topic. For example, discuss: With so many denominations, how can believers still see themselves as one Body of Christ? How can diverse denominations work together to further the mission of the kingdom of God?

Digging Deeper

Handbook of Denominations in the United States, 12th Ed. by Craig D. Atwood (Abingdon Press, 2005).

The Complete Guide to Christian Denominations: Understanding the History, Beliefs, Differences by Ron Rhodes (Harvest House, 2005)

See also www.religionfacts.com/christianity/denominations.htm

Worksheet Key

(1) b (2) e (3) c (4) a (5) g (6) h (7) d (8) f (9) j (10) i

© 2010 Rose Publishing. www.rose-publishing.com. Permission granted to reproduce for classroom use only. Taken from Rose Bible Basics: What Christians Believe #772X ISBN:9781596364141

CHAPTER 6: BAPTISM

Main Idea

Baptism is an important part of the Christian faith, but Christian groups practice baptism differently.

Teaching Tips

Prior to this session research your church's/denomination's official view of baptism. Is baptism part of their statement of faith? What Scriptures do they use to explain their stance on baptism? Is baptism required for church membership or leadership? Share this with the group.

Remember that the topic of baptism can be controversial. For many people, their baptism—or their children's baptism—is a meaningful and personal event in their life. Some participants may be believers who have not been baptized. In expressing the importance of baptism for Christians, be careful avoid sounding accusatory or causing them doubt their salvation. Instead, focus on the experience and blessing of baptism in a Christian's life, as well as Jesus' command to be baptized.

Digging Deeper

Understanding Four Views on Baptism, Baptist View by Thomas J. Nettles, Reformed View by Richard L. Pratt, Jr., Lutheran View by Robert Kolb, Churches of Christ View by John D. Castelein (Zondervan, 2007)

"A Celebration of Baptism" in *Desiring God* podcast by John Piper. Makes the case for believer's baptism. Audio file available for free at http://www.desiringgod.org/ResourceLibrary/sermons/bydate/1982/342_A_Celebration_of_Baptism/

Worksheet Key

(1) False   (2) False   (3) d   (4) e   (5) True

CHAPTER 7: UNDERSTANDING THE BOOK OF REVELATION

Main Idea

The book of Revelation provides hope and encouragement for all believers, although believers may interpret the book in different ways.

Teaching Tips

Open the session by reading Revelation 1:1–8, John's opening words. Explain that from the beginning of the book the focus is on the "Lord God and Jesus Christ our savior," and that is what needs to be kept in mind as one reads Revelation. This will help set the tone for the session, keeping the focus on God and the truth that Scripture is God's revelation to us so that we might glorify him.

Key questions to consider: (1) Are the Old Testament promises and covenants for all believers today, or only for the people of Israel? (2) Should we look more to the blessings of the future, or here on earth? (3) Are the promises in Revelation only for believers, or for all people? How a person answers these questions conditions how he or she reads the book of Revelation.

Digging Deeper

Four Views of the End Times pamphlet (Rose Publishing). Diagrams comparing four views on the millennium.

© 2010 Rose Publishing. www-rose-publishing.com. Permission granted to reproduce for classroom use only. Taken from Rose Bible Basics: What Christians Believe #772X ISBN:9781596364141

Three views on the Rapture, Pretribulation by Paul D. Feinberg, Midtribulation by Gleason L. Archer, Posttribulation by Douglas J. Moo (Zondervan, 1996)

Four Views on the Book of Revelation, Preterist by Kenneth L. Gentry Jr., Idealist by Sam Hamstra Jr., Progressive Dispensationalist by C. Marvin Pate, Classical Dispensationalist by Robert L. Thomas (Zondervan, 1998)

Worksheet Key
(1) historicist   (2) futurist   (3) idealist   (4) preterist   (5) futurist

CHAPTER 8: WHAT'S SO GREAT ABOUT HEAVEN
Main Idea
Heaven is at the heart of God's plan for creation; It's all we ever dreamt of and more.

Teaching Tips
The issue of near-death experiences may arise during group discussion or teaching time. If it does, remind participants: (1) It is difficult to know what is happening in the unconscious mind during medical/physical trauma, so we should not be quick to rely on every near-death experience story; (2) Always compare personal testimonies against what Scripture says; and (3) Focus on what we *do* know about heaven that has been revealed in the Bible.

Digging Deeper
"What Will Heaven Be Like?" by Peter Kreeft (6/1/03), available at www.christianitytoday.com/ct/2003/juneweb-only/6-2-51.0.html

Heaven: Your Real Home by Joni Erickson Tada (Zondervan, 1997)

Surprised by Hope: Rethinking Heaven, the Resurrection, and the Mission of the Church by N.T. Wright (Harper One, 2008).

Journey into the Light: Exploring Near-Death Experiences by Richard Abanes (Baker, 1996).

Worksheet Key
(1) False   (2) False   (3) e   (4) c   (5) True

Feedback
To improve future studies, be sure to get feedback from the group about teaching style, meeting location, discussion time, material covered, length of study, and group size. Choose a method that best suits your group: Anonymous evaluation sheet, e-mail response or questionnaire, open discussion. (See the feedback questions at the end of the study guide.)

The inclusion of a work or website does not necessarily mean endorsement of all its contents or of other works by the same author(s).

STUDY GUIDE

The study guide which begins on the following page includes a reproducible worksheet and/or discussion questions for group discussion or personal reflection.

© 2010 Rose Publishing. www.rose-publishing.com. Permission granted to reproduce for classroom use only. Taken from Rose Bible Basics: What Christians Believe #772X   ISBN:9781596364141

Essential Doctrine Made Easy

Worksheet

Fill in the blanks.

Essential Doctrine:

#1. There is only one _____.

#2. God is one essence, but three _____.

#3. We are sinful and cannot please God by our own _____ _____ alone.

#4. Jesus became a _____ _____ through supernatural conception in Mary's womb.

#5. Jesus was _____. Thus he is able to represent us before God.

#6. Jesus Christ is, in essence, _____.

#7. Jesus Christ was fully _____, as well as fully divine.

#8. God—and God alone— is able to _____ us.

#9. Faith, not _____, connects us to God.

#10. Only Christ's sinless life, sacrificial _____, and bodily resurrection can bring us to God.

#11. Jesus rose _____ from the grave.

#12. _____ ascended, body and soul, to God.

#13. Christ _____ our best interests before God.

#14. Jesus is _____ again soon, and we should be ready.

Discussion Questions

1. Which essential doctrines do you think are easiest for people to accept, and which ones most difficult? Why?
2. How does understanding the "bad news" of human depravity, help us appreciate the "good news" of Jesus?
3. How does learning more about the Christian faith affect one's walk with God?
4. What is God's promise to believers for the future?
5. What is the significance of Jesus' resurrection?
6. If someone were to ask you, "What is grace?" what would you say?

© 2010 Rose Publishing. www-rose-publishing.com. Permission granted to reproduce for classroom use only. Taken from Rose Bible Basics: What Christians Believe #772X ISBN:9781596364141

Creeds and Heresies: Then & Now

Worksheet

1. What are creeds?
    a. Basic, memorable statements of essential Christian belief.
    b. Statements that join Christians in unity in "one Lord."
    c. Statements that help believers identify false teaching.
    d. All of the above
    e. None of the above

2. Doctrine is from the Latin word *doctrina* meaning:
    a. Healing or health
    b. I believe
    c. Teaching or learning
    d. Acknowledge

3. Which is <u>not</u> true of Gnosticism?
    a. The material world is evil—and an illusion.
    b. It is seen in much of today's pop spirituality.
    c. It's a form of pantheism.
    d. God and his creation are separate.

4. True or False? The Apostles' Creed was written by the apostles not long after they completed the four Gospels.

5. True or False? Creeds help Christians articulate how their beliefs differ from other teachings.

Discussion Questions

1. Does your church use creeds? If so, in what way?
2. How do creeds help unify believers?
3. What stood out to you as you read the section on heresies in early church history?
4. Why was defending the deity of Jesus so important to the early church?
5. What are the creeds relationship to the Bible? Should believers treat them differently or the same?

© 2010 Rose Publishing. www-rose-publishing.com. Permission granted to reproduce for classroom use only. Taken from Rose Bible Basics: What Christians Believe #772X ISBN:9781596364141

The Trinity

Worksheet

Look up each Scripture passage below and list all the attributes and activities described. (Some are already begun for you.)

Attributes and Activities

Father

Psalm 100:3 — *Creator. Owner of us. Authority over his creation.*

1 John 3:20

Psalm 138:3

Genesis 1:1

Ephesians 1:4–5

Jeremiah 23:24

Romans 16:25–27

John 5:21

Son

Colossians 1:16–17 — *All creation through him. Without him nothing could exist. Supreme.*

John 5:21

Revelation 1:17–18

John 1:4

John 21:17

Philippians 4:13

Ephesians 1:22–23

Romans 8:10

Matthew 8:31–32

Holy Spirit

1 Corinthians 2:10–11 — *Knows the deep things of God. Reveals the things of God. The Spirit of God.*

Hebrews 9:14

1 Corinthians 12:11

Ephesians 3:16

Psalm 139:7

Psalm 104:30

Romans 8:11

Compare all three lists. What similar attributes and activities do you notice across all three? What does this tell us about God the Father, the Son, and the Holy Spirit?

© 2010 Rose Publishing. www-rose-publishing.com. Permission granted to reproduce for classroom use only. Taken from Rose Bible Basics: What Christians Believe #772X ISBN:9781596364141

The Trinity

Discussion Questions

1. After reading this chapter, what did you learn about the Trinity that you previously didn't know or misunderstood?
2. Why is Jesus' divinity important for our relationship with God?
3. The three Persons of the Trinity are in relationship with one another. Does God existing in relationship make a difference in how we should live? Why or why not?
4. What are some practical things you can do to help you relate to God as triune—Father, Son, and Holy Spirit?
5. What questions do you still have about the Trinity and would like to learn more about?

© 2010 Rose Publishing. www.rose-publishing.com. Permission granted to reproduce for classroom use only. Taken from Rose Bible Basics: What Christians Believe #772X ISBN:9781596364141

Life of Jesus

Worksheet

1. True or False? Jesus was human while on earth and became divine after his resurrection.

2. Which is part of Jesus' message?
   - a. Repentance
   - b. Belief
   - c. Himself
   - d. (a) and (b)
   - e. All of the above

3. Jesus referred to himself in the Gospels as:
   - a. The gate
   - b. The bread
   - c. The book
   - d. (a) and (b)
   - e. All of the above

4. True or False? Jesus' betrayal and execution came as a surprise to Jesus.

5. Which of the following is *true* about Jesus' second coming?
   - a. Jesus did not speak of it while on earth
   - b. Only believers will see him when he returns
   - c. Only believers will rule with him
   - d. (b) and (c)

Discussion Questions

1. Books and movies portray Jesus in many ways: Jesus the revolutionary, Jesus the martyr, Jesus the rabbi, Jesus meek and mild, Jesus the healer, etc. How do you view Jesus when you read the Gospels?
2. When Jesus preached that the "kingdom of God is near" (Mark 1:15), what might his first-century Jewish audience have understood it to mean? What do you think people today understand it to mean?
3. What does it mean that Jesus was the *Christ,* the *Messiah?* How do people nowadays understand these terms?
4. In what ways did Jesus' resurrection change the lives of his disciples? How does it change the lives of believers today?

© 2010 Rose Publishing. www-rose-publishing.com. Permission granted to reproduce for classroom use only. Taken from Rose Bible Basics: What Christians Believe #772X ISBN:9781596364141

Denominations Comparison

Worksheet

Match the following terms with their descriptions. (Use each only once)

1. ____congregational
2. ____inerrant
3. ____evangelical
4. ____catholic
5. ____Pope
6. ____liturgical
7. ____immersion
8. ____orthodox
9. ____Calvinism
10. ____Apocrypha

a. Literally, "universal." The faithful church in all its expressions worldwide.

b. A form of church government in which each local church is self-governing; practiced by many denominational groups.

c. Conservative Christians, mostly Protestant, who affirm the infallibility or inerrancy of the Bible.

d. A form of baptism in which a person is completely submerged under water; nearly always practiced in Baptist churches.

e. Without error; used by evangelicals with reference to the complete trustworthiness of the Bible in all matters on which it speaks.

f. Adhering to the essentials of the Christian faith, especially as articulated in the early creeds.

g. The title, meaning "Father," referring to the Bishop of Rome (head of the Roman Catholic Church).

h. A form of corporate worship in which the priest or minister leads the congregation in readings and prayers from a prescribed text.

i. Books considered part of the Old Testament in Catholic or Orthodox theology but not in Protestant theology (e.g., 1 and 2 Maccabees, Wisdom of Solomon).

j. The theological tradition particularly in the Reformed and Presbyterian church bodies.

Discussion Questions

1. What did you learn from this chapter that you didn't know or misunderstood before?
2. Are you more familiar with liturgical or non-liturgical churches? If both, how was your experience in liturgical and non-liturgical churches different and similar?
3. How important is denominational affiliation in your family or among your Christian friends? How important is denominational affiliation to you?
4. What do you think are some reasons for why there are so many different denominations?
5. The apostle Paul says in Ephesians 4:25 that believers are "all members of one body." How do you understand this in light of so many denominations?

© 2010 Rose Publishing. www.rose-publishing.com. Permission granted to reproduce for classroom use only. Taken from Rose Bible Basics: What Christians Believe #772X ISBN:9781596364141

Baptism

Worksheet

1. True or False? Those who practice infant baptism believe that the act of baptism itself saves a person.

2. True or False? The debate over baptism for believers vs. infants first began during the Protestant Reformation.

3. Which of the following was *not* emphasized as a part of baptism in church history?
    a. Initiation
    b. Identification
    c. Infusion
    d. Individuation

4. Believer's baptism:
    a. Is usually practiced by immersion.
    b. Emphasizes faith as a human response to God's grace.
    c. Closer to the Old Testament model of sacrifice, than circumcision.
    d. (a) and (b)
    e. All of the above

5. True or False? Initiation in baptism refers to entering into the life of Christ's body.

Discussion Questions
1. What did you learn about baptism from this chapter that you didn't know or misunderstood before?
2. What types of baptism services have you attended or been part of? Share your experience in the different types.
3. Why is baptism important in a believer's life? Is baptism mandatory for believers?
4. In what ways is baptism a corporate (or community) act, rather than just an individual act?

© 2010 Rose Publishing. www-rose-publishing.com. Permission granted to reproduce for classroom use only. Taken from Rose Bible Basics: What Christians Believe #772X ISBN:9781596364141

Understanding the Book of Revelation

Worksheet

Fill in the blanks using the four views below (may be used more than once).

Historicist   Preterist   Futurist   Idealist

1. In the _____ view, the events in Revelation are seen as symbolic descriptions of historical events throughout history.

2. In the _____ view, nearly all of Revelation is yet to occur.

3. Only the _____ view does *not* see the book of Revelation as prophetic.

4. In the partial _____ view, most of Revelation is prophecy fulfilled in the first century AD, though final chapters of Revelation describe future events to occur at the end of time.

5. Dispensationalist premillennialists (and some historic premillennialists) interpret Revelation in the _____ way.

Discussion Questions

1. What stood out to you as you read this chapter?
2. Which view are you most familiar with? Which view are you least familiar with?
3. When you read the book of Revelation which of the four approaches do you typically take?
4. How does a person's view on the book of Revelation change how they see God's plan for the future?
5. The apostle Paul writes in 2 Timothy 3:16 that "all Scripture is ... useful for teaching, rebuking, correcting and training in righteousness." In what ways do you see the book of Revelation being useful for believers today?

© 2010 Rose Publishing. www-rose-publishing.com. Permission granted to reproduce for classroom use only. Taken from Rose Bible Basics: What Christians Believe #772X ISBN:9781596364141

What's So Great about Heaven

Worksheet

1. True of False? The physical world is evil, so we must focus on the spiritual which is good.

2. True of False? None of the features of this world will continue in the renewed creation.

3. Which of the following will end in the renewed creation?
   a. Marriage
   b. Death
   c. Work
   d. All of the above
   e. (a) and (b)

4. In heaven we will worship God always; This means that we will all:
   a. Sing hymns day and night.
   b. Be in church every day.
   c. Have an attitude of awe, gratitude, humility, and love.
   d. Be really bored.

5. True or False? Christ is the first example or "firstfruits" of all who will be raised into new life.

Discussion Questions

1. What do you remember learning about heaven when you were growing up?
2. At what times in your life do you most reflect on the afterlife? Give an example.
3. In what ways does having a belief in the reality of heaven change the way we live our lives now?
4. How can a person be sure that he or she will go to heaven?
5. What questions do you still have about heaven and would like to learn more about?

© 2010 Rose Publishing. www-rose-publishing.com. Permission granted to reproduce for classroom use only. Taken from Rose Bible Basics: What Christians Believe #772X ISBN:9781596364141

FEEDBACK

1. What did you learn through this study that deepened your relationship with God and/or helped you understand biblical teachings better?

_____

_____

2. What was your favorite thing about this study, and why?

_____

_____

3. How could the meeting location, setting, length, or time be improved?

_____

_____

4. Did you think the material covered was too difficult, too easy, or just right?

_____

_____

5. What would you like to see different about the group discussions?

_____

_____

6. What would you like to see different about the activities?

_____

_____

7. What topic would you like to learn more about?

_____

_____

© 2010 Rose Publishing. www-rose-publishing.com. Permission granted to reproduce for classroom use only. Taken from Rose Bible Basics: What Christians Believe #772X ISBN:9781596364141

MORE Rose Bible Basics

Why Trust the Bible?
Is the Bible an ancient document that has been tampered with? Has it been edited many times over the centuries and now is filled with errors? How can we know what the Bible really said when the originals no longer exist? 128 pages ISBN: 9781596362017

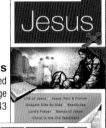

Jesus
This easy-to-understand book provides a biblically centered approach to learning who Jesus is and why his powerful message of salvation matters today. 128 pages, ISBN: 9781596363243

Christianity, Cults & Religions
This book clarifies the differences between the beliefs and practices of various religions, cults, and new religious movements. Includes topics such as: Who is God? Who is Jesus Christ? What is salvation? What happens after death? 128 pages ISBN: 9781596362024

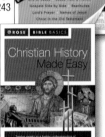

Christian History Made Easy
This easy-to-read book brings to life the most important events and people in Christian history that every believer should know. 224 pages, ISBN: 9781596363281

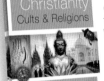

Names of God and Other Bible Studies
Contains favorite Bible studies to use in small groups, church groups, and for individual study. 128 pages ISBN: 9781596362031

God in Real Life
To navigate life's tough choices, teens and young adults need a real relationship with God in their real life. This book provides clear, biblical answers to their questions. 128 pages, ISBN: 9781596363250

Where to Find It in the Bible
Handy, full-color companion for Bible study and teaching. Helps you locate: • Your favorite Bible verses by topic • 100 prayers in the Bible • Important people of the Bible • 100 prophecies fulfilled by Jesus • 52 key Bible stories

Provides a one-year Bible reading plan, basics of Bible study, and a harmony of the Gospels. 128 pages ISBN: 9781596363441

The Bible at a Glance
This full-color book is an introduction to basic Bible knowledge. Contains a Bible overview summarizing each book of the Bible, a Bible time line comparing Bible history and world history side by side, steps to studying the Bible, Then & Now Bible maps, and more. 128 pages ISBN: 9781596362000

Myth-Busters
This full-color book covers important topics everyone faces: atheism, evolution, reliability of the Bible, historical evidence for Jesus, and the teachings of "spiritual" leaders today. Helps you engage these popular issues with clarity and solid facts. Great for youth and adults. 128 pages ISBN: 9781596363458

Free, downloadable study guide at rose-publishing.com.
Click on "News & Info," then on "Downloads."

Other Rose Publishing Books

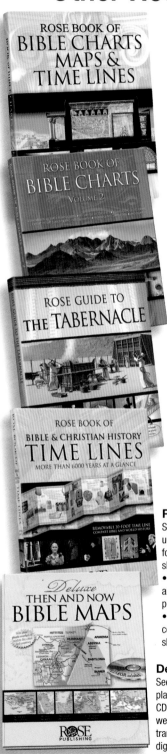

Rose Book of Bible Charts, Maps & Time Lines

Dozens of popular Rose Publishing Bible charts, maps, and time lines in one spiral-bound book. Reproduce up to 300 copies of any chart free of charge.

- Christianity, Cults & Religions
- Denominations Comparison
- Christian History Time Line
- How We Got the Bible
- Tabernacle
- Temple and High Priest
- Islam and Christianity
- Jesus' Genealogy
- Bible Time Line
- Bible Bookcase
- Bible Overview
- Ark of the Covenant
- Bible maps
- Trinity, and more.

192 pages. Hardcover.   ISBN-13: 9781596360228

Rose Book of Bible Charts 2

Here are dozens of popular Rose charts in one book! Topics include • Bible Translations comparison chart • Why Trust the Bible? • Heroes of the Old Testament • Women of the Bible • Life of Paul • Christ in the Old Testament • Christ in the Passover • Names of Jesus • Beatitudes • Lord's Prayer • Where to Find Favorite Bible Verses • Christianity and Eastern Religions • Worldviews Comparison • 10 Q & A on Mormonism/Jehovah's Witnesses/Magic/Atheism and many others! Hardcover with a spine covering a spiral binding. 240 pages ISBN: 9781596362758

Rose Guide to the Tabernacle

Full color with clear overlays and reproducible pages

The Tabernacle ("tent of meeting") was the place where the Israelites worshiped God after the Exodus. Learn how the sacrifices, utensils, and even the structure of the tabernacle were designed to show us something about God. See the parallels between the Old Testament sacrifices and priests' duties, and Jesus' service as the perfect sacrifice and perfect high priest. See how:

- The Tabernacle was built • The sacrifices pointed Jesus Christ • The design of the tent revealed God's holiness and humanity's need for God • The Ark of the Covenant was at the center of worship. Clear plastic overlays show inside/outside of the tabernacle; plus dozens of reproducible charts. You may reproduce up to 300 copies of any chart free of charge for your classroom. 128 pages.ISBN: 9781596362765

Rose Book of Bible & Christian History Time Lines

Six thousand years and 20 feet of time lines in one hard-bound cover! This unique resource allows you to easily store and reference two time lines in book form. These gorgeous time lines printed on heavy chart paper, can also be slipped out of their binding and posted in a hallway or large room for full effect.

- The 10-foot Bible Time Line compares Scriptural events with world history and Middle East history. Shows hundreds of facts; includes dates of kings, prophets, battles, and key events.
- The 10-foot Christian History Time Line begins with the life of Jesus and continues to the present day. Includes key people and events that all Christians should know. Hardcover. ISBN-13: 9781596360846

Deluxe "Then and Now" Bible Maps Book with CD-ROM!

See where Bible places are today with "Then and Now" Bible maps with clear plastic overlays of modern cities and countries. This deluxe edition comes with a CD-ROM that gives you a JPG of each map to use in your own Bible material as well as PDFs of each map and overlay to create your own handouts or overhead transparencies. PowerPoint fans can create their own presentations with these digitized maps. Hardcover. ISBN-13: 9781596361638